Dealing with Dealers

Jeremy Cooper

Dealing

with

Dealers

The Ins and Outs
of the London
Antiques Trade

Drawings by Julie Hoehn

Thames and Hudson

First published in Great Britain in 1985
Reprinted 1985

Printed and Bound in Great Britain by
Billing and Sons Ltd., Worcester.

Contents

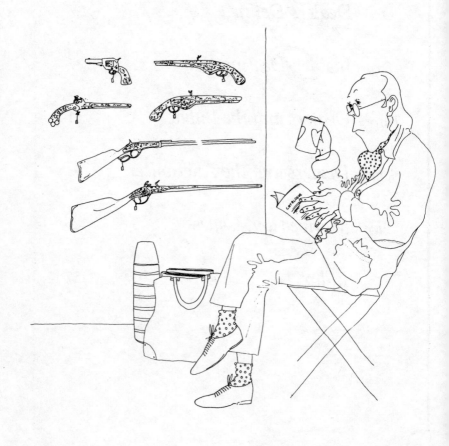

— *One* —

Dealers Defined

While antique dealing lacks the status of a profession, it is looked upon as a highly acceptable occupation, more profitable than the church, less reactionary than the army, and much more amusing to talk about than stock-broking.

In earlier generations a few dealers became respected public figures either through commercial success, such as Lord Duveen, or through their scholarship and expertise, like Dominic Colnaghi. Social acceptability on this grand scale, however, was limited in the art market to purveyors of the Fine Arts – pictures, sculpture, drawings, prints and antiquities, subjects with an academic pedigree. The antique dealer who trades, by definition, in the Decorative Arts (furniture, ceramics, silver and the rest) was treated with suspicion.

No longer.

Collecting is the craze of fashionable society, and London hostesses pay regular homage to their favourite antique dealers and decorators.

'Antiques', and thereby antique dealers, have become fashionable largely because of a widespread feeling of dissatisfaction with all things modern. Opinion has it in Mayfair and Knightsbridge that new furniture, new ceramics, new silver, new almost-everything is less valuable and inferior to old almost-anything. Respect for the past is rife. Chairs to sit on and cups to drink from need not be terminally old, but they must not be new. Definition of an antique as an object more than one hundred years old no longer applies, for many established dealers take pride in the fact that nothing in their shops predates the Art Nouveau period. The 1950s revival has already begun. Second-hand approaches the height of fashion.

Before the Second World War collecting works of art was a relatively restricted activity in England: an enclosed world inhabited by rich eccentrics and a limited number of dealers, mostly in established family businesses. These dedicated and essentially secretive collectors still exist, as do the specialist dealers serving their interests, but the antiques trade as a whole expands and broadens in response to the demands of an ever-widening public following. The media play a crucial role in bringing antiques into the public eye. Price guides, dictionaries of antiques, and collecting magazines roll off the presses despite recession in other areas of publishing, and television promotes furniture experts into national gurus. This popularizing of antiques has led to the diversification of good taste. With more buyers chasing a decreasing number of genuine pieces, objects consigned yesterday to charity stalls reappear today in Chelsea shop windows.

This makes for a healthy and fast-moving market place but it creates difficulties of definition. Whereas it was comparatively easy to define collecting taste in the 1880s, as exhibited in the Sotheby's auction of the contents of Mentmore Towers in 1977, it is more difficult to extract the typical taste of the 1980s. Before investigating the operations of the London antiques trade, it is sensible to establish first the kind of works of art that a rich and fashionable collector might buy today; for it is the fashionable goods that are the most expensive and around which the structure of the antiques trade is built. Without a clear picture of this it is impossible to understand the workings of dealers' rings, 'running', 'knocking', and other intricacies of the trade.

What antiques do the Hon. George Everyman, a successful merchant banker, and his Bostonian wife have in their London home?

To begin with, the typical house of the rich collector of today is not a newly constructed mansion projecting into the Buckinghamshire landscape like Mentmore Towers. Disapprobrium for modern artefacts extends to modern architecture, and today's collector of taste lives in a large Victorian townhouse in the vicinity of Holland Park, lovingly renovated and judiciously modernized in line with current preservationist dogma. Furthermore, even the avowedly independent collector is unlikely to have escaped the clutches of a leading decorator; not only the colour of his walls and the texture of his fabrics will have been chosen for him, but many of the works of art he has collected will reflect the style of the all-powerful decorator. Not that Mayer de Rothschild furnished Mentmore without help; agents and dealers scoured Europe for appropriate embellishments to grace the Baron's new home – a fireplace from Rubens's house in Antwerp, multi-coloured marble busts from Rome, and iron shiploads of eighteenth-century furniture from French châteaux. Yet Rothschild was permitted to do a good deal of shopping on his own in Oxford Street, and Mentmore boasted much brand-new and ultra-modern furniture and fitments among the antiques. The 1980s man of fashion must limit himself in things modern to concealed lighting, concealed video, concealed security, and perspex-and-steel coffee tables.

Within this anti-contemporary framework, the choice of approved antiques for the Holland Park house is wide and attractively eclectic. They are all available in the London trade, despite a challenge from New York still the centre of the world antiques market, and the Hon. and Mrs Everyman shop far and wide, from market stalls in Bermondsey early on Friday mornings to the lush emporia of the West End.

Virtually all the furniture they have bought in the last fifteen years is hard-edged and architectural with none of the rococo curves of the Mentmore era of collecting. Instead of a Louis XV giltwood canape with cut-velvet upholstery, there is a Regency black-and-gilt settee in beige horsehair, the arms carved with inventive Egyptianesque detail. The German boie-claire pier-tables and secretaire work well with the heavier taste of the English pieces, and the Palais Royale mother-of-pearl and ormolu ornaments add a luxurious note. Mrs Everyman, with her energetic eye for a bargain, picked up the mother-of-pearl tazza in one of her favourite shops on the Kings Road, past World's End, before it could work its way through the trade to Bond Street and into the hands of a rich Iranian. Another of the Everymans' discoveries is a mahogany desk chair published in 1807 by Thomas Hope, a stunning piece of design and craftsmanship. The centrepiece of the library is a rosewood centre table with brass and tortoiseshell inlay within veneered malachite borders made in the 1820s by George Bullock. A few years ago the furniture designs of Bullock were virtually unknown, but the publication of academic articles has led to keen competition among museums for his pieces; the Hon. George Everyman bought his Bullock table in Mount Street where he was forced to pay 'a museum price' for it. Overlooking the Japanese-style garden, the upstairs sitting-room is entirely furnished in Art Deco – contrasting screens by Eileen Gray and Pierre Legrain, chairs by Jean Dunand, and a large collection of Décorchement glass in ebony display cabinets. The room, as recorded in photographs for *Connoisseur*, is dominated by a Ruhlmann baby-grand piano from the Paris Exposition of 1925, bought in 1978 at a cost approaching £100,000. High fashion only occasionally comes cheap.

For the dining room almost anything goes in the 1980s, except Chippendale and Hepplewhite which are both far too reactionary in taste for the refined collector. The Everymans' first idea was to create the effect of a garden terrace with Tiepolesque frescoes, old mirrors with peeling mercury, and a tented ceiling; they went so far as to buy a pair of crystal-glass throne chairs from a Hyderabad princeling and, from the Pimlico Road, a rare eighteenth-century fernwork sideboard. In the end they decided on a less ephemeral scheme: Titian-red walls and vast Charles the Second portraits hanging in their original frames from brass rods, a bold sideboard possibly designed by William Kent, and a set of 1740s Irish chairs. The dining table is a masterpiece of reconstruction – pedantic concern for the original form and function of works of art is rejected by trend-setters in interior design – the black slate top being made from six Victorian wash-stands banded in coloured marbles looted from a seventeenth-century specimen cabinet, the steel frame supported at each end on the backs of Assyrian granite lions and at the centre on a first-century BC Corinthian capital.

Having restrained themselves in the dining room, the Everymans ran riot in the downstairs cloakroom, the walls and ceilings of which are encrusted with sea-shells in architectural patterns drawn from Mannerist grottoes. The hand basin is an antique marble bird-bath with a Paul de Lamerie silvergilt dish for the soap, the water emerging from the mouth of a bronze Bacchus mask (remnant of a fountain in one of the Barberini palaces in the Campagna). In order to avoid the use of modern taps, the water is controlled by a rubber pad in the floor, as in railway carriages. As there was no way to disguise the lavatory itself, the Everymans' decorator felt it best to leave the original Victorian cistern, now also encrusted with shells, and to install an antique mahogany box-commode.

In the early 1980s, though modern was still abhorred, proto-modern received the official stamp of approval. Scattered among the Regency pieces, and looking slightly out of place in the comfortable proportions of the Victorian architecture, are a pair of Mackintosh crescent-back chairs first made in 1897 for Miss Cranston's Tea-Rooms in Glasgow. Mrs Everyman is proud of these as she bought them at auction in London 'against the trade' for only £3,000, half the asking price for a single chair in a specialist dealer's in Belgravia. Such a good client is Mrs Everyman that no one in the trade dare point out that her Mackintosh bargains are second-hand Cassina reproductions. The shelf full of Hoffmann metalwork is appropriately housed in a Koloman Moser cabinet. Also displayed in the drawing room is a small collection of Linthorpe pottery designed by Christopher Dresser in the 1880s but looking, with its bold shapes and amazing glazes, more like the 1930s. Impressed by the opening of the Boiler Room at the Victoria and Albert Museum, Mrs Everyman is keen on replacing her Harrod's upholstery with some 1950s Charles Eames chairs; she is also thinking of Alvar Aalto cantilever chairs, but her husband cannot remove from his mind the idea that all this stuff is no more than discarded office equipment, not 'art' at

all, much less 'antiques'. He needs reminding that the antiques market has always been a place for reassessment – in the 1960s Tiffany lamps now worth $100,000 were difficult to give away; in the 1930s Burne-Jones tapestries sold for less than the artist had been paid for designing them fifty years before; in the 1890s Regency sofa-tables were banished to the maid's room; in the 1850s Louis XV was 'in' and Elizabethan 'out'; and in the sixteenth century Italian sculptors were commissioned to refashion ancient Roman statues to make them look more Greek.

Today's collectors tend to be less interested in Oriental ceramics than were their fathers and grandfathers. The only things which the Hon. George has kept from his family's extensive collection are the plain-coloured Sung pieces and a selection of celadon ware which the decorator chose in order to set off the marbleizing in the bathroom. Everyman's own Oriental purchasing concentrates on the Persian and Turkish as opposed to the Chinese and Japanese, perhaps because merchant bankers these days spend more time in Islamic than in Buddhist countries. Just as imperial conquest influenced the taste of nations in the nineteenth century (witness the impact of Egypt on Napoleonic taste, and of India on Victorian), so commercial expansion in the twentieth century alters our visual point-of-view. In the Holland

Park house are to be found a beautiful series of Persian bowls and vases decorated with bird and animal silhouettes and a collection of sixteenth-century Isnic tiles, the bold iron-red of which was a popular colour in the 1970s (*cf.* Ryman filing cabinets, Braun kitchen units, and Habitat coffee mugs).

The basement of this double-fronted Victorian house has been opened up at the back into a huge kitchen-living room, and at the front into a photographic studio for the Everymans' eldest son. Such is the attraction of things old that the Aga cooking range has seen a revival and a modern version of this traditional apparatus faces an oak refectory table and a French provincial buffet covered with majolica in all shapes and sizes – bright green lettuce-leaf plates, delicious strawberry dishes, animalistic tureens, and mad monkey teapots. A stripped-pine dresser, the one near the medieval stained-glass windows leading on to the patio with cast-iron furniture and coadestone planters, contains the blue-and-white collection, English domestic ware of the late eighteenth and early nineteenth centuries which Mrs Everyman collected while her children were still at school and there was less money available for investment in antiques. It was also before she could afford her decorator, who smartly turned her away from blue-and-white and towards wooden

decoy ducks, African tribal art, sextants, and Anglo-Indian memorabilia. The refectory table was bought on the decorator's advice from one of the select band of dealers whom he favours; both dealer and decorator agreed vociferously that the table was 'definitely right' and 'absolutely period', while neglecting to divulge from which period they considered it to be so 'right'.

It is difficult to take everything in on the first visit to the typical house of the typical collector of taste, for his home is crammed with works of art. The Everymans' textiles are particularly impressive, so wide-ranging in origin and of high quality – a Susani panel hanging in the drawing room, exquisitely embroidered with uneven colours and asymmetric patterns as protection against the evil eye; a group of Coptic fragments on the staircase, away from direct sunlight; a restrained Amish quilt in the guest bedroom, the pattern formed not in colour but in complex stitchery; and some Elizabethan crewel-work in the main bedroom, including a magnificent covered glovebox with the monogram of Bess of Hardwick. After seeing the pioneering Gianbologna exhibition at the Victoria and Albert in 1978, George Everyman decided to hedge himself against inflation within sixteenth- and seventeenth-century bronzes. His collection is growing rapidly. While on holiday in Tuscany last year he acquired a Gianbologna toad from the Ouspensky collection which was paid for in Switzerland and delivered to him in Holland Park by a mysterious intermediary. The Hon. George was rather annoyed when the editor of *Connoisseur* insisted that the expensive toad be photographed in the jacuzzi, away from its habitual spotlight splendour on the Bullock table.

And there is so much else besides, some works of art which always were and always will be well-considered, others which have moved in and out of fashion over the years, and too many which are aesthetically admired today but will never be sought after again as anything more than historical curiosities.

The sources available in the London antiques trade to collectors such as the Everymans are best described in their several separate categories, in descending order of prestige.

First to the West End Emporium. Having passed inspection by the lady seated at the Louis Quinze desk near the door, one enters a world of diverse works of art with titled connections, of copperplate cards with poetic descriptions, and of prices on request. A multitude of riches for the multi-rich. The stock may be arranged through six or seven immaculate rooms with prices totalling several million pounds; in such places the mark-up of selling price over cost price must average more than 100 per cent just to break even, for the overheads are as fabulous as the prices. A front-of-house staff of five or six is supported by the same number of restorers in full-time employment plus a cricket team of cleaners, van-drivers and bookkeepers. And the establishment running costs quickly escalate into hundreds of thousands of pounds a year with West End rates, rents and upkeep of de luxe premises, weighty advertising campaigns, world-wide travel expenses and the endless other costs of efficient dealing on the grand scale.

At whatever level he may operate, the central problem for the serious dealer is first to locate the right kind of goods and then to find the money to purchase them. Once you have them, the best things more or less sell themselves. Like any other retail business, commercial success in antique dealing thus rests on good cash-flow, a notoriously difficult task in a trade which fluctuates on so many levels beyond the individual's control, and failure at which can lead to bankruptcy in no time. The small man tends to look jealously upon the prestigious West End Emporium, assuming that the money will always be available to buy the best goods where lie the best profits. In reality the aristocrats of the trade have the financial problems of the parvenu writ large. It takes a nerve of ormolu to maintain exclusive control over Giles Grendey bureau-bookcases or Cressent commodes by buying another one at £90,000 when the two already in stock have remained unsold for a couple of years. A matter of fine judgment, judgment of works of art and of the market, judgment made on experience and expertise.

However, the established West End dealer has earned himself certain advantages. On the strength of a financial track record, extensive borrowing is normally available in lean times, either from the bank or from private backers; and there are the masterpieces to call upon which all dealers bury away in the privacy of their own homes. It is a truism of the trade that the unseen item, the rarity which has not appeared in the market place for decades, perhaps for centuries, is worth twice as much as a piece of similar importance fresh in the memory from a recent auction. Through contacts with old clients and access to family collections, the leading West End dealers are able to acquire such works of art privately and it is a delight to see the apparently endless succession of unknown rarities which they muster. It is this which gives them their power in the market, for where else can the millionaire go, acquisitive and impatient with time, to furnish his new Mayfair home in the style demanded of his self-importance. In a year or two such a client may spend a million pounds, maybe three, at the West End Emporium which can give him all that he wants. The by-no-means-apocryphal Arab has been known to spend the same in a day – the work of a super-salesman in tweed hacking jacket on a Monday morning, hot-foot from a weekend in the country.

Next in line of succession in the trade hierarchy come the large general specialists, the fine English furniture dealers, the Oriental ceramics and works of art dealers, and the major *objets de vertu* dealers – denizens of the West End, of Knightsbridge, of Kensington and of the smarter end of the Fulham Road, members to a man and a woman of the British Antique Dealers' Association, defenders of the old-fashioned pre-1830 dateline, and standard-bearers in the free trade campaign. They see themselves as the official voice of the antiques trade; they are pen-pals with the editor of *The Times* and lobbyists of the House of Commons. 'Save Our National Heritage' they cry when arguing for the sale of their most expensive piece to a British museum; 'Export Antiques and Earn Dollars' they cry if asking for a licence to export the same piece to an American museum.

This close-knit group of dealers is the mainstay of the London auction rooms. Most of the traditional-taste antiques appearing every week in the London rooms are bought by members of this clan, which exerts considerable control on the market. Their aim is to maintain in stock a wide choice of good quality eighteenth-century objects which are turned over relatively quickly; they are therefore ready to buy any number of Hester Bateman teapots at the right price, or Hans Sloane botanical plates, or Chippendale pie-crust tripod tables, or *famille rose* vases, or any of the other acceptable if slightly dull works of art which have been the staple diet of the trade for generations. The Fulham Road furniture dealer of repute unable to show a prospective client at least three Regency sofa-tables at a couple of thousand pounds or so each would be severely embar-rassed. He would leap into his maroon Volvo Estate and accelerate away to replenish his stock. While he is away his brother (or cousin or wife or son) may well sell two Georgian bookcases, three sets of sabre-legged dining chairs, and a collection of tortoiseshell tea-caddies to a peroxide blonde dealer from Florida on one of her quarterly buying trips to Europe; and it's back into the Volvo for another scout around the auction rooms.

Large shops set out with safe antiques lit by table lamps with bottle-green shades or housed on top-light glass shelves, permanently dust-free. The fragrance of freshly cut flowers fighting off the smell of furniture polish. Soft-voiced people treading mustard-coloured carpets and trading on the confidence of conservatism. Nothing much has changed over the years beyond the imperceptible pushing forward of the datelines, from Georgian, to Regency, to William IV – anything but Victorian, a word which, if ever passing the lips of a member of the clan, is pronounced in the same tone as Lady Bracknell exclaiming 'A handbag!?' in *The Importance of Being Earnest*. One shop is much like the other, each dealer interchangeable with his mates, honest, knowledgeable, unobjectionable and unexceptional; like English furniture in 'The Age of Mahogany', so much more decorous and restrained than the gilded vulgarities of the continentals. These qualities are appreciated today as much as they ever were; they form the solid centre of the London trade.

The narrow, rather than the general, specialists are a more varied, idiosyncratic group of individuals, less easy to categorize in sweeping generalizations. For them success depends not on fashionable appearances nor on traditional good taste but on their knowledge and enthusiasm for their chosen subjects. Survival as a specialist dealer rests on the ability to discover unrecognized rarities through apprecia-tion of the subtleties of artists, craftsmen and manufacturers

from forgotten cultures and neglected fields. Whether the subject be mechanical musical instruments, Byzantine ivories or Tyrolean treen the expertise of the top-line specialist cannot be faked. It is a business which only suits people for whom working life and private life are inseparable, people who are more interested in the objects they handle than in anything else in the world. To outsiders they may be cranks or bores or both, but to collectors, fellow specialists and to academics in the field they are the salt of the earth.

The size and scope of specialist businesses range from market stall plus gladstone bag to West End shop plus company van; in between these two extremes many specialists these days take space in the smart Antiques Markets, a London development of the last decade to counter escalating rents and rates. Some specialists may be difficult to track down in hidden arcades and, once found, may frighten the neophyte unused to confronting dealers perched on stools in tiny cubicles festooned with antique surgical instruments, theatrical ephemera, mourning jewellery or whatever else their fetish might be. To those genuinely interested in the subject the contact is always worth making, for ten minutes' chat over an object is more informative than hours studying any book on collecting.

Whatever they are and whatever image they present to the public, most specialists operate with their own money in an independent and personally identifiable way. Nevertheless, all such businesses have certain things in common. In the first place, the supply of goods comes substantially from within the trade. Every good dealer has an eye for quality (and for profit) in an object outside his field which he may come across at a country auction or in his round of regular calls. He may not have an outlet for it himself, but word-of-mouth leads him to the specialist in that field and to a sale, providing there is 'enough left in it' for the specialist. You learn early on in the trade not to begrudge the next man his profit. A certain amount also comes from auction where the specialist is treated with respect by the general dealer. If the leading expert in engraved glass is not bidding on a rare example, the non-specialist tends to assume either that the glass is not as rare as it appears to be or that the known collectors already have an example and there is no profit at the auctioneer's reserve

price. The intricacies of these tacit understandings between dealer and dealer will be discussed in detail in a later chapter, but, as a general rule, interference by a non-specialist in an esoteric market leads to disaster. The basic reason for this is that the specialist of standing has an international network of customers whose needs and foibles he knows well, and it takes years for a young dealer, however dedicated to his subject, to build up a business to rival the existing specialist sitting in the middle of his spider's web with dozens of captive flies kept alive by regular feeding of collecting rarities. Or, looking at it another way, collectors are like drug addicts, the dealer like a drug pedlar hooking his client onto rarer and more costly works of art. The supply of rarities is necessarily limited and the market is controlled by the leading specialists.

Certain specialist dealers maintain a low profile, their shops somewhat forbidding to the casual passerby, their selling mostly on the telephone, not over the counter. Others seek to interest new collectors by mounting public exhibitions with weighty catalogues. A dealer may have to hoard stock for ten years in preparation for such an exhibition and lay out a further £15,000 to mount the show and print the catalogue; scarcely a purely commercial proposition, but for such dealers it is part of the pleasure of the business and an enjoyable way of making a reputation. An alternative method, available only to those with academic contacts, is to build up within their stock a rounded collection of a particular subject and sell this in a single deal to a museum, an investor or an 'instant' collector. This also takes time as the collection must, arguably, be unrepeatable and will usually be built on the back of an existing collection; such foundation collections are difficult to obtain as they are normally inherited property which the auctioneers compete for, aiming to split the collection up into separate lots. Even if the specialist has the financial power to remove the collection from the hands of an auction house he still has to fill in the gaps and find a rich client.

If not necessarily the most profitable part of the antiques market, specialist dealing is entertaining and creative. As well as being characterful it is also highly risible as specialists, like dog-lovers, develop some of the physical attributes of the works of art they cherish. There is the early English pottery dealer as bemused and amusing as the quirky things he sells, his head stuffed with historical anecdotes and teeth ever ready to bite into the neck of a figure and test repair. And the Art Deco sculpture dealer, angular in mind and body, longing to be asked to pull on gold tights and leap across the stage.

Among the London specialists, silver dealers and carpet dealers are the most clannish in their habits and the most antagonistic to outside rivalry. Emerging from their underground vaults in Chancery Lane, silver dealers follow each other like ants along the routine paths to and from the London auction rooms. There is an unwritten, unalterable ritual in viewing a silver sale: in rhythmic movements the half-spectacles are pushed to the end of the nose, the silver salver removed from the case, the warm breath exhaled over the silver mark, the pocket magnifying glass placed to the eye and returned to the pocket, the salver weighed in hook scales, and the ritual completed by coded marking of the catalogue. These actions are accompanied by banter between silver dealers which is intelligible to none but themselves.

Carpet dealers reserve their tribal dance for the auction itself. The full complexities of the Anglo-Armenian carpet dance have not been seen in London since the auction rooms began to clip the rugs onto racks and to hang the carpets on the walls instead of piling them up at the back of the room where the dance developed its classical form in the 1960s and early 1970s. It was a marvelous sight. The leader

of each performance was to be identified by a red carnation, a bowler hat, or long black coat with astrakhan collar; he and the six principal dancers skipped back and forth across the carpet gesticulating to each other and to their partners crouching at the side counting the stitches. Each section of the dance ended with the leader raising his hand, or the stub of his cigar, to the auctioneer; and another carpet was rolled back for inspection. After twenty or thirty lots of carpets the air at the back of the auction room was so heavy with the dust of country houses and the sweat of the performers that the dancers invariably removed themselves to the street pavement or to a nearby café to complete the tribal ritual in secret.

The next section of the trade comprises the dealer-decorators and decorator-dealers, a group of considerable influence despite the fact that not all its members are instantly identifiable. Of course, the appearance of folders of fabric samples on a chaise longue and wallpaper books in a canterbury immediately marks certain decorator-dealers. But all dealer-decorators' shops look much like any other

smart general antique shop – until, that is, one looks closely at the objects themselves and discovers that they are no longer individual works of art and have become mere accessories to the decorative ambience. The signs are all there for the critical eye to see. More cushions than chairs. The decoration of lustre bowls hidden by piles of sea-shells or rose-petals. Overmantels as bed-heads, bed-heads as boiserie, boiserie as picture frames, picture frames as overmantels. Shepherds' smocks mounted in perspex and hung on the wall. A fine Queen Anne bureau bookcase with a mahogany cornice; a Meissen chinoiserie teapot with a pewter lid.

The best decorators, those who are entrusted with the refurbishment of fine houses belonging to people with little time but some taste, are often good dealers as well and can be relied upon to supply decent works of art at acceptable prices. Many good dealers are also excellent advisers to their clients on the choice of a colour scheme for the dining room or on the design of curtains for the drawing room. It is the dealer-decorators and decorator-dealers in the business of supplying instant fashion who cannot be admired. Then, neither can one admire the people who want instant fashion, people who seek in a matter of months to give the impression that their newly-acquired Chelsea house or Bayswater mews or Mayfair flat has existed in such colourful contrived chaos for generations.

Next, to the private dealer, who has no fixed place in the trade hierarchy. At one end of the scale he is the man with a first-floor suite in Old Bond Street supplying millions of pounds' worth of arms (antique) and armour to the Metropolitan Museum, the Sheikh of Muscat, and the freebond warehouses in Zurich. In the middle of the scale she is the lady in a large terrace house in Putney from whom collectors in California and dealers in Knightsbridge buy their best Ruskin vases and Doulton figurines. At the bottom of the scale he and she are the couple who have nothing better to do with their time and money than wander about the salerooms buying bits and pieces for their various houses and selling them on to acquaintances.

It is becoming increasingly attractive for a successful dealer to close down his shop and set up a by-appointment business. The main reason for having a shop is to spread the disease of collecting to new victims, but it is a time-consuming and costly activity involving fixed opening-hours, extra staff, high rents and overheads, constant security problems, and wasted hours of idle chatter. Once a dealer is established in his field, profitable business can best be done on the end of a telephone to selected clients, or, for the real high roller, by telex and Concorde. There are a limited number of buyers in the world for the great rarity at the top price and once reputation and experience have introduced a dealer to these potential purchasers he no longer needs a shop to advertise his wares. Many of the largest deals in the art market are conducted from start to finish behind closed doors, the names of buyer, seller and dealer never being known to the public, nor to the taxman. Private dealers need sell no more than half a dozen works of art a year to make an exceedingly good living, indeed one deal can be enough for a lifetime's supply of caviar and chorus girls. In antique dealing dreams often come true, but only those dreams built on the reality of deep knowledge, hard-won international reputation, cool marketing and ceaseless research.

Closely connected with the private dealer is a new breed, the art market agent and consultant. He is the broker of the trade, the fixer. It is a difficult job, for although the consultant does not risk capital in purchasing stock he has substantial office overheads which can only be recovered by a percentage charged on successful deals. The trouble is that the consultant tends to be given the impossible commissions: to find a buyer for the star lot at auction which failed to reach its reserve; to obtain an exorbitant price for a minor work by a major artist; to acquire an entire Gothic library of documented Pugin furniture; to dispose of a collection of pornographic snuff boxes to a single buyer for a quarter of a million dollars, payment in the Dutch Antilles, collection in Hong Kong.

The need for brokerage in the art market arose in Western Europe and in the United States during the 1970s partly to conceal the sale and acquisition of works of art from wealth-tax-threatening governments, partly because auctioneers were no longer trusted as middlemen in view of purchasing activity on their own account, and partly to service portfolio investment in works of art. Some consultants are renegades from the leading auction houses, others are ex-curators of wealthy private collectors, and many are rich, well-connected dilettantes with a reputation for good taste. If the reputation is justified then the latter are the best agents to use, as they have money enough of their own not to be tempted by bribery from the seller on top of their commission from the buyer.

A substantial section of the antiques market is controlled by 'Trade Only' dealers and their allies the warehouse exporters. From modest premises in Notting Hill several dealers achieve turnovers of over a million pounds a year in furniture, clocks and decorative objects; many warehouses in unfashionable areas of London dispatch a container load a week of 'brown furniture' across the world to clients who pay for the goods unseen in advance.

Certain dealers who place those 'Trade Only' signs in their windows maintain a fine stock which would be of interest to many collectors; but though such dealers often have genuine feelings for works of art they do not like people. Excuses will be found – that the bookkeeping and Value Added Tax returns are less onerous when selling for export or to registered English dealers; that they do not have the time to write descriptive labels and prices on the stock; that with goods piled to the ceiling in their small shops, there is no room for beguiling browsers; that the public are unreliable payers, complain about the condition, and three weeks later change their mind and insist on having their money back. All true – yet truer is the fact that these men and women are locked into their own narrow world of regular faces and familiar objects and do not wish to meet challenge or change.

Known euphemistically as 'the boys', these dealers work hard for their money and live modestly. In a sense they form the most professional section of the antiques trade, operating on tight cash-flow and treating works of art as a commodity just like any other retail trader. Not for them the pretensions of some antique dealers who shun the term trader and think of themselves as curators of culture. Some of the boys seem to be mistrustful of the money they made during the 1970s boom in antiques and continue their habitual pattern of a seven-day working week including the Portobello Road on Saturdays and antiques fairs on Sundays. They are cautious buyers. When one of the boys views a sale he looks carefully at every lot, notes the condition in his catalogue and puts a coded price on everything. Before attending the auction the next day he will have worked out at precisely what price he will sell each piece, what the costs of restoration and transport are likely to be, and how much he is prepared to bid, allowing for a higher potential profit on those goods which experience tells him will take longer to sell. The boys are immune from auction fever, they are far too professional.

The warehouse exporters buy antiques at Christheby's in much the same way wholesalers buy vegetables at New Covent Garden: Victorian mahogany and walnut per square foot, East Anglian tomatoes and cauliflower per kilo. Whether vegetables or antiques, the value of each part of the container load depends on quality, condition and rarity. Bow-front chests of drawers are worth more than straight ones, and more still with their original handles. Bulls-eye barometers are hot sellers in Miami, early radishes in Paris, and they are priced accordingly, the biggest consignments being put together by the dealer with the most efficient marketing organization.

In London the small general dealer with the corner shop selling 'Antiques and Curios' and repairing clocks or framing pictures as a side-line is being pushed out of business. The vast increase of interest over the last twenty years in collecting has sent prices beyond the reach of his ambitions and of his abilities. If he is lucky he will have sold his lease at a decent price to the Kentucky Fried Chicken chain and bought a Tudor cottage in the main street of Lavenham where tourists still bring a living to the general dealer. He cannot tell whether the horse brasses in the local auction are original or not, and he does not know that his Georgian bureau was made in the reign of George the Sixth not the Third, but none of this matters as all the lady from Sydney wants is a memento from Suffolk. She does not care if it is old, it just has to look 'olde'. A few traditional antique shops survive on long-standing leases in London villages like Primrose Hill and Greenwich, but most of the general dealers who have stayed in town now operate alongside the small specialists in the Antiques Market complexes. They seem to do it as much for the companionship of like-minded people as for the profit. One looks after the other's pitch when there are grandchildren to mind at home, and they buy and sell among themselves when customers are scarce. They read auction reports rather than go to sales, sort out the world's problems within smelling distance of the next cup of coffee, and are charmingly attentive to every enquiry.

Down near the bottom of the dealers' pecking order though he may be, the open-market stallholder is held in more respect by the professionals than are many shop-owners. Too many businesses in all areas of the antiques trade are run by people who have made their living by other means and will always remain amateurs as dealers. Most stallholders who turn up before dawn at Bermondsey Market on Friday mornings are full-time professionals who drive hundreds of miles a week buying goods for the London trade. For many it is their main outlet and business is brisk as no one wants to cart dud stock around in the back of a van all week. There are twenty London dealers standing around the stall of one of the dozen best market traders as he unpacks his haul from battered suitcases and groaning luggage rack. Within half an hour several thousand pounds in notes disappears into the top pocket of the stallholder and off he goes for a Victorian-sized breakfast, leaving a hench-man behind to flog the dross.

As in all social orders, the man at the foot of the scale has the easiest access to the man at the top. 'Runners', dealers with nowhere to display their goods other than the roof of their cars, sell more works of art to the West End Emporium than anyone else in the trade. After all, the pavement is nearer than the nearest shop and while the rain may be an inconvenience the emporium's doorman holds a brolly over his boss and the runner cuts his price as the rain threatens the tortoiseshell inlay on the rosewood table he is offering. And the runner? He has his freedom – no overheads, no hours, no stock, no staff, no tax. The Hon. and Mrs Everyman own quite a few works of art which started out life in the London antiques trade on top of our runner's car. He does not mind the fact that there may be a nought on the end of the price the Everymans paid the emporium for the much admired Bullock centre table; our runner spends more time than any of them do in his own home enjoying many wonderful works of art which are not yet fashionable.

Two

Insider-Dealing

Most dealers do most of their selling to other dealers. The precise balance of trade and private business varies, narrow specialists selling much more than the average to private collectors, perhaps 50 per cent of their turnover, while others do all their business with fellow dealers. In boom times the dominance of insider-dealing means that the antiques trade comes dangerously close to turning in entirely on itself with works of art passing back and forth between stock-hungry dealers at ever-increasing prices and never finding their way out of the trade-maze into the hands of a private buyer. It is hardly surprising that antiques are so expensive when half-a-dozen profits are involved in transferring a Bow figure from an estate in Exeter to a collector in Salisbury. In this way, antique dealers are like children at a birthday party playing 'Pass the Parcel' as they hustle their latest purchase down the road to the next shop before the music stops. This insider-dealing seems to be part habit, part business acumen, and part paranoia, the antique trade's perpetual fear that the bubble will burst. Looked at less benignly, the trade is an incestuous family of parasites feeding off the remains of past generations and creating nothing but their own dead money.

In order to understand the peculiar practice of insider-dealing it would be interesting to ring two antiques, like a naturalist studying geese, and follow them in their migration across the trade from the breeding grounds in Bermondsey Market and the secondary sale-rooms to safety on the shores of a fine collection.

Firstly, an enamel pendant in the shape of a swan which appeared one morning on a stall in Bermondsey. The stallholder had bought it the day before at an auction in East Anglia, part of the contents of a bashed box of nicknacks; he had not bothered to clean it up and the pendant was an unappealing sight to the non-professional eye. Not so to the trade, and as soon as he unpacked his gladstone bag several hands reached out for the swan.

The stallholder intercepted the covetous hands and passed the pendant over to one of his regulars who had asked before grabbing, a costume-jewellery dealer in Charlie's Antique Market who queued at the stall every Friday morning waiting for the unloading ceremony. He spent several hundred pounds most weeks, stocking up for the lazier traders in Charlie's who preferred to give him a profit rather than get up early themselves. He turned the pendant over in his hand, rubbed it on his sleeve, and asked the price. The stallholder was busy with another customer, knocking out seven gold bangles at less than melt value, and did not reply. The dealer offered a price of £20 which was summarily rejected with protestations from the stallholder that it was worth 'a ton of anyone's money and cheap at that'. After an inconclusive argument as to whether or not it was gold, £40 exchanged hands and the little pendant disappeared into the dealer's inside pocket alongside his other purchases.

Five minutes later, as he walked away from the stall, a young man wearing an ankle-length leather coat fell into step at his side and tried to persuade him to pass the swan on immediately for a £15 profit. The offer was refused. Half an hour later the young man appeared at his side again and simply held out four unused £20 notes. The dealer thought for a moment, took the notes and handed over the pendant. Even if it did clean up well, he reckoned he was unlikely to get more than that for it at Charlie's.

It was before dawn on the swan's first day out in the open market and already two dealers had made a profit on its migration.

The new owner was the fourth generation of an unambitious family of Chancery Lane Silver Vault dealers, where he worked for his father. The swan had reminded him of the magnificent productions of Victorian goldsmiths such as Antonio Cortelazzo from Vicenza, and he had hopes of a high reward for his early morning exertions. He hurried home to dip the swan in chloride and smarten it up a bit before unveiling the discovery to his father over the breakfast table.

But the mount was so deeply encrusted with dirt that no casual cleaning could bring it up and it had to be passed over to the restorer in Hatton Garden. On collecting it, the young man was somewhat relieved to find that it was indeed gold, with a London assay mark for 1866 on the clasp. The quality of the enamel, however, seemed disappointing, the pitted surfaces having none of the translucent brilliance of the Cortelazzo workshops. The inexperienced dealer did not know quite what to do, for he was unsure of the swan's value and did not know anyone whose advice he trusted in such matters – certainly not his father's, whose automatic habit of overvaluing his own stock and under-valuing everyone else's was too deeply ingrained to change now. In the end he made 'the mistake of asking an in-between price of £250 which had the effect of arousing the suspicions of his potential customers in the trade. After he had offered the pendant unsuccessfully to his father and to three other dealers in the Vaults the market for his erstwhile 'coup' was exhausted, and three weeks later he was happy to take £150 for it from an *objets de vertu* man in the Bond Street Arcade.

The next owner wisely decided to work out exactly what the enamel pendant was, and therefore what it was worth, before trying to sell it. The first puzzle to solve was the date of 1866 on the ring-clasp which did not match with the possible dates of the enamel; nineteenth-century enamels of this type are almost always technically flawless and the dealer felt that this robust swan must either be a twentieth-century reproduction or, more optimistically, a much earlier original. On examination beneath a powerful microscope it became clear that the Victorian clasp was made in a different carat gold from the body of the swan, and had been painstakingly and expensively applied, presumably in the 1860s, soon after the clasp was made. This implied that the swan was already an old and valued possession in the Victorian period, but exactly how old was difficult to ascertain. Further than this the man in the Arcade could not go, for his speciality was Russian not European enamels and there was no way he could substantiate his belief that he had been lucky enough to purchase an original Elizabethan enamel of the kind shown in Holbein's portraits of court life.

Best to ring up one of the large specialists round the corner in Bruton Street, and do a deal.

The telephone conversation followed the standard pattern, social greetings over in a moment and down to business – an arcade dealer does not ring a leading impresario of the trade without having something to offer. The big man's two main concerns were the provenance (family history) of the swan and the question of whether it had been seen by anyone else in the trade. By 'anyone else' he meant one of his three or four rivals in London; the small man gave assurances that 'no one else had seen it', which was true because he always brought such things to his best contact first, knowing how valuable it was to produce stock fresh for collectors. The seller was nevertheless firm in his refusal to discuss a price until their meeting, which was arranged for the following afternoon.

The arcade dealer smiled to himself as he put down the telephone. The bait was cast. Now, what should he ask? The answer to that question depended on an assessment of the eventual selling price – with support for a sixteenth-century attribution from a contact in the museum world, an asking price of well over £2,000 would not be out of the question, so he decided to pitch his opening throw at £1,000 and accept £750 if forced to. No point in being too greedy on such a speedy turnover.

Over a pot of mint tea the next afternoon a bargain was struck without too much trouble and they shook hands on a deal at £850 on condition that the Victoria and Albert Museum expert was prepared to give his verbal opinion in

the enamel's favour. One of the Assistant Keepers called round later in the week, and over lunch at the Golden Guinea gave the enamel positive vetting. Two weeks after that the swan appeared in the Bruton Street window nesting on a black satin cushion, all signs of the Victorian clasp having been carefully removed; the asking price, on application, was £2,800. And despite the covetous attention of one American and two Greek collectors, there it stayed for nearly two years because doubts lingered on in everyone's mind about the true age of the swan with his fine white chest and flashing ruby eye.

Then a Jermyn Street specialist, while researching on the collections of the Dukes of Rochester, came across an engraving of the swan pendant in an 1811 catalogue of the Duke's collection which gave its full history back to 1592. Needless to say, he kept this piece of information to himself until he had negotiated the purchase of the swan from his rival for a bargain price of £1,500. Now that the swan boasted a ducal pedigree the new owner had no difficulty in finding a buyer at over £4,000, and the Tudor swan completed its migration by flying off to a deposit box in Fort Lauderdale.

This all happened several years ago; prices have since changed but the principle has not. Last month a set of ten Gothic Revival dining chairs made their migration across the London antiques trade in much the same way.

The chairs, with wide caned seats and low arched backs, surfaced at a secondary salesroom in West Kensington during August when many dealers are away on holiday. Long sets of chairs are good sellers and a private dealer from Sydenham was grateful for the lack of competition, picking them up for £450, less than £50 a chair. He did not even try to sell them and merely piled them up at the back of his garage, confident that the first of his regulars to return from holiday would take them on at £700 without any argument. He was right, and off they went to a dealer in Highgate who touched in the scratch marks with stain and gave them a heavy polish before putting them in his shop window marked at £1,400, 'trade price' £1,200. As often happens they were bought by a dealer at a higher level of the trade who had different ideas about how the chairs should look and they went straight off to the restorers for recaning and to have the stain and polish stripped off to the natural pollard oak, waxed to a warm honey colour. Fitted out with squab cushions in sky blue silk, they looked sensational on their reappearance in a Kensington Church Street window where they were instantly spotted by the director of a West End Emporium while driving past on his way to a dinner party. On the telephone the next day the director was surprised by the 'best price' of £4,000 for a set of chairs which were, after all, only Victorian even if, for the sake of decorum, they were called William IV. The only way forward was to borrow a couple to show to a client, and as the Emporium asked their client £6,000 for the set there was much to-ing and fro-ing before the deal was completed. The chairs then ended their migration in the smart dining room of a country house in Wiltshire, a mile or two from the M4 Motorway.

Outsiders find it curious that this well-known chain of insider-dealing has not been broken either by energetic private buyers or by independent, anarchic dealers. There is a great deal of money to be made, it would seem, by the dealer who can buy at the beginning of the chain and sell at the end, thus taking three or four people's profits as his own. Equally, there must be money to be saved by the dedicated collector with time to spare in scouring the sources rather than waiting till things filter through to the West End at inflated prices. One might even expect more dealers themselves to object to this undistinguished way of earning a living, and yet it still goes on with only a few imaginative dealers and collectors leaping the chain.

Yet the London antiques trade is a sophisticated business which handles billions of pounds worth of goods every year and one must look for more solid commercial reasons for its structure other than its simply being a lazy way of making money.

The most cogent commercial argument for insider-dealing is that it solves one of the dealer's most difficult problems, cash-flow. Most dealers are wildly undercapitalized, and with prices moving ever upwards the only way they can stay in business is to spend more money than they actually have and rely on passing the goods along in the trade relatively quickly. Prices can move so fast that a fine William Morris carpet, for example, may be sold very profitably for £5,000 and twelve months later may cost the dealer £8,000 to replace in his stock. In such circumstances, if a dealer is to stay in the market and reap the profit of his expertise in a booming field, he is forced to borrow money in order to replenish stock and good cash-flow is essential in order to service the interest on his debts. So, although a certain amount of insider-dealing occurs as a result of mistakes, as in the case of the swan pendant, in most cases the underselling to another dealer at less than the full retail value is deliberate.

In areas outside a dealer's own speciality works of art are passed around the trade knowingly at prices considerably below their full value because only the top specialists know the private clients who will pay the top prices, and many dealers cannot afford to wait five or six months for a suitable auction, where a high price is not guaranteed anyway. From attending auctions and from keeping his nose to the wind a good dealer knows the 'worth' of a large range of works of art and will buy outside his field if the prices are cheap enough. The good dealer also knows, however, that a recorded price of £1,000 at auction for an Art Deco this or a Russian that does not make a similar example he buys for £100 worth any more then he paid for it until he finds someone to buy it from him. Works of art have no intrinsic worth, no list value, they are worth exactly what anyone pays for them at any one time. Young hopefuls in the trade soon discover that the best profits are made from what one's own clients want, not what someone else's do. So, better than sitting out for a high price on something outside one's field and possibly not getting it for a year or more, better by far to sell it on immediately to another dealer for £300, an excellent percentage profit, and use the money to buy something else on which another quick profit can be made. Good cash-flow is essential in every way, not least for the freedom it gives a dealer to be prepared for the masterpiece in his field when it turns up – there is nothing more aggravating for a dealer than to witness a great rarity in his field selling relatively cheaply at auction when he has no money with which to bid.

There is, of course, more to insider-dealing than simply the management of financial resources. Buying and selling between dealers is not only a way of making money, it is part of the way of life of a dealer, it is an expression of relationships within the trade. Relationships and personal contacts are the essence of good dealing.

The dark side of insider-dealing is this incestuous chain of profits at the expense of the private buyer. The bright side is the building up of relationships between dealer and dealer

whereby the desired work of art makes its way to the right collector for whom its possession means so much. The successful completion of this process depends on the sharing of information and pooling of resources which occur between friends in the trade. This is how a living is earned in those antique shops where a customer seldom opens the door to disturb the tobacco parliament conducted round a desk near the back of the room at which three of four men can be seen drinking coffee, making and receiving interminable telephone calls in various languages, and plotting among themselves. Only one of the smokers works in the shop, the others have left 'the girl' to run their shops while they 'do the rounds'. For many dealers, doing the rounds is not only an excuse for the twice-weekly fix of nicotine-stained gossip; it is the means by which vital information is gathered and money is made. Each dealer helps himself and his friends in a variety of ways during these regular sessions; in that sense dealers are like freemasons operating a closed order of mutual self-protection.

It is surprising to discover how often rival specialists share their knowledge and opinions with colleagues without any direct financial benefit to the man providing information on his rival's stock. This is partly a good specialist's irrepressible interest in the subject itself which sends him scurrying to reference books and research files to provide precise historical details on a rare object. It is also the pleasure which any dealer with genuine regard for his subject obtains from discussing and analyzing the qualities of a work of art with another expert – even if that expert is his commercial rival and the pleasurable feelings are accompanied by intense jealousy at the other's possession of a masterpiece. Anyway, an enthusiastic chat about a fine object gives a useful boost to the confidence, and selling works of art is all about confidence – confidence in one's own judgment, confidence in the stability of the market, and confidence in the inherent merits of the object itself.

It is, one must remember, a tiny world and specialist dealers know almost all of each other's clients. Living as many do off the same collectors, everyone is interested in keeping the richest of these collectors happily involved in the market. So dealers spend a good deal of time discussing how they can satisfy the tastes of individual clients and prevent them from obtaining things cheaply from other sources. Collectors do not realize how often the praise showered on an expensive tit-bit in a rival shop is not altruistic admiration at all but subtle persuasion to buy something in which the dealer has a secret half-share. Similarly dealers may excuse their underbidding of an object at auction against a client with the claim that they were obliged to execute a commission bid for another client when there was in fact no such bid and they were merely protecting the price structure. Different circles of dealers nurture their own groups of clients and try to maintain a uniform approach to them, particularly avoiding offering the same things at vastly differing prices. Rich collectors are afraid of a volatile market and there are numerous examples of collectors deserting the field altogether as a result of uneven pricing or uncertainty due to the appearance of fakes in the auction rooms and the trade; good dealers work together to protect their clients from the vagaries of the market and from the dishonesty of others. Dealers also work together to protect themselves from bad clients. There is a constant exchange of information about which foreign dealers and shipping agents are unreliable in the settling of their accounts, about which collectors expect large discounts and should therefore be quoted a higher asking price, or about which so-called experts are time-wasting windbags.

This all sounds and is professional, difficult, and not a little devious. Despite the complexity of these kinds of arrangements, more time is spent by the same people in rambling discussions about the state of the market than on any other topic of conversation. 'How's business?' is on the tip of every dealer's tongue and no one seems to tire of the interminable ramifications of answering this question. As no dealer is prepared to admit that he is doing well – for fear of his suppliers putting their prices up – these conversations tend to follow a repetitive course of complaints about rising overheads, moans about the high prices collectors are prepared to pay at auction and not in the shops, and disgust at the low quality of goods on the market. Prophecies of doom are frequent, the saving solution most often promoted being to buy the best and nothing else. This is a solution open only to a tiny percentage of dealers, for few of them have the knowledge to recognize the best when they see it, unless it is highlighted by a colour plate in an auction catalogue, by which time it will be too expensive for them to buy. And to whom could they sell it anyway? It is not as simple as the top men make it appear.

General chatter about the state of the market then turns to specific discussion of prices. Again the tone is often of whinging pessimism and of nostalgia for the days when everything could apparently be bought 'for a song'. Buying with hindsight is so much easier, and dealers are often to be overheard talking about the times when Pre-Raphaelite pictures were a few hundred pounds each and Gallé glass cost less than three-figure sums; if only they had not, like almost everyone else, dismissed as rubbish such present-day stars of the market. Some dealers complain about everything – about someone paying too much for a bronze at auction and alerting people to the value of that particular sculptor's work; about the prices a rival pays the runners, thus opening their eyes to the vast profits made out of them by others; about auctioneers, about journalists, about the government, and about clients, above all their own clients.

The specialists complain least about the market because they are the most organized in the control of its forces. When an unusual collection in an esoteric field appears on the market the three or four leading specialists usually get to hear about it immediately, and often meet to work out a strategy for its joint purchase. The luckless dealer, facing the united front of the specialists with no alternative outlet of his own, will be forced to accept a knock-down price. A collection once bought by a group of specialists can then be split among their several shops and sold on a uniformly high price structure which eager collectors have no choice but to accept. It is a clever game played for high stakes, the winnings at which are a closely guarded secret – another reason why many dealers are unwilling to put prices on their stock, to conceal from both suppliers and potential competitors what the ultimate selling price might be.

While 'doing the rounds' friendly dealers also discuss the possible selling prices of each other's newly-acquired stock. 'How much do you think that vase could stand?' is the customary phrase. So many variables come into play in the pricing of works of art that constructive advice from friends in the trade is invaluable; this advice is readily available for the reason that dealers do so much buying and selling among themselves that money made in one shop is often spent in another. The pricing of a great rarity is entirely a matter of personal opinion, but with standard works of art there are methods of appraisal which can lead to a more or less unchallengeable fair market price. Take, for example, a Kang Hsi blue and white baluster vase.

An expert eye can quickly establish that there are no peculiarities in the reign mark or in the iconography of the decoration which might catapult an outwardly ordinary object into the price-category of a rarity. This established, the first point on which a judgment has to be made concerns the degree of the vase's appeal in a purely decorative sense. Certain tones of blue, consistencies of glaze, subjects of painting, and proportions of baluster are considered more decorative than others; and the right combination of charac-teristics makes the vase more desirable to many more people and therefore perhaps twice as valuable as a vase with the wrong combination of colours, glazes, etc. Then there are market matters to consider – whether there is too much or too little similar material available in the London market, whether or not the export market to Hong Kong is buoyant, and whether the pound is strong or weak compared to the dollar. And finally the decision as to what price to ask depends on how much a specific client, trade or private, might be willing to pay for it, and how desperate the dealer is to make a sale.

After the coffee and the biscuits, and the cigarettes and the chatter, actual business begins with a question, put as casually as possible, like: 'Well, what is the very best you could do for me on that console table in the corner?' If the dealers have built up a good relationship over several years of doing business together, the conversation could then take many different directions. The table may be a recent purchase and with no one else specifically in mind for it the dealer may decide to pass it on to his colleague at a 30 per cent mark-up, which could be half of the labeled price. On the other hand, if the table was bought cheaply and the marked price is a reasonable one, the dealer may prefer to hold out for a discount of no more than 20 per cent (the standard 'trade terms' of 10 per cent discount is available to almost anyone and the negotiating factor is normally much higher between dealers who do business together regularly). On the most expensive items an outright purchase is not expected from a dealer-friend at the same level in a similar type of business, and, if the visiting dealer thinks he may have a client for the table, various alternative arrangements can be investigated. The simplest method is to send the client in to buy the table direct and for an agreed sum to be reserved within the selling price for the man who made the introduction. But if the client is a big spender one dealer will not want to put him in touch with a rival, and the more likely arrangement is for the table to be consigned at an agreed net price to the owner, leaving the second dealer free to make whatever profit he chooses to on top. However, some dealers are chary of consigning stock except as a last resort, because another dealer is naturally keener on selling his own stock, which is tying up his own money, than persuading his clients to consider someone else's objects. The normal though more complicated method is for the second dealer to buy a half share in the table at a price which already gives the first dealer a small proportional profit and leaves the remaining profit till his colleague sells the table, a task he will approach with greater energy having invested working capital in his share.

Similar arrangements are made between runners and dealers who know and trust each other, especially when the runner realizes what he has and what it is worth, and threatens to put it into an auction. It could easily happen that a runner buys a Gordon Russell sideboard for £60 in a country sale where the auctioneer and all the other dealers fail to spot the significance of the piece, because the handwritten labels of early Gordon Russell furniture are pasted on the underside of the drawers. A good runner will know that the specialist charges over £1,000 for such pieces and that a reserve of £600 would be accepted by one of the leading auction houses in an Arts and Crafts sale. The runner may therefore ask £600, an acceptable price if the specialist has the money and the space. Yet the trade is full of sharp-eyed, profit-conscious people, and Gordon Russell furniture could not be bought as cheaply as it often is unless there was a good commercial reason. The reason is clear – there are very few collectors and it is therefore very difficult to sell; it is, if you like, a name for the future. So the specialist might sensibly reply that the most he is prepared to pay outright for the sideboard is £300, but he would consider buying a half share of the runner's cost price and splitting the sale price fifty-fifty. The runner will probably tell a small fib and say the sideboard cost him £100, take £50 for a half share from the specialist and look forward to another £500 or so when it is sold. The specialist is also happy, because he makes the same profit as he would have done if he had bought it outright at £600 but has to lay out only £50.

The last task of a dealer on his rounds is to discover by surreptitious questioning whether his rivals have spotted anything of interest coming up for auction in the country the following week. It is a double game of cat-and-mouse, the aim being to catch the other dealer's discoveries while preventing him from catching yours. The game, more often than not, ends in a draw, with both parties accepting the fact that they have each spotted the same thing and that they might as well go to the sale in one car and save petrol.

Success in antique dealing depends, for many, on building up these relationships within the trade, and the hours and hours of chatter are, like oil to a motor-car, essential to the mechanics of insider-dealing. Not, one would have thought, a suitable job for the solitary introvert; yet some independent dealers manage to do well for themselves without entering the tangled undergrowth of insider-dealing, a fact which leads one to suspect that those who do lead such a life positively enjoy the intrigue and claustrophobia. It may be that the antiques trade works as it does not through any inherent commercial necessity, but merely because the majority of dealers prefer it that way.

The antiques trade is not one in which the public expect any protection from either the written law or any unwritten code of conduct; it is country laid with mines and money-traps – 'Danger. Buyer Beware'. Despite the new-found respectability of certain dealers and decorators in fashionable London circles, the wider public reaction to the trade is founded on mistrust and dislike. In a recent documentary film an antique dealer was seen beating the interviewer to the pavement with an iron bar after it was proved conclusively that everything in his shop was fake. 'Typical of antique dealers and second-hand car salesmen,' commented the *Neasden Weekly News*. Though the deals are seldom as criminal or as dangerous as some people think, the antiques trade is not a model of blamelessness. Yet, like many closed communities where external laws have little control, there is a relatively strict internal code of behaviour which is enforced by genteel variations of gangland justice.

The cornerstone of the internal law of the trade is the rule 'No Comment'. The reason why there is virtually no legal case history concerning antiques dealing and auctioneering is the long established practice in the trade of solving disagreements privately, not through the law courts. This practice is founded on the belief that if the trade refuses to comment to the press or to the public then there can be no evidence and no case; it is part of a self-perpetuating conspiracy of silence. As it is almost impossible for a dealer to avoid becoming involved in some way with the potentially compromising machinations of the trade, everyone tends to become tied to the established code of behaviour. This is why nothing is known by the public at large, and little more has been discovered by journalistic investigation or government enquiry about the precise workings of the antiques trade. It is all a very secretive business in which billions of untaxed and unrecorded dollars are pushed about the world in the confidence that no one will divulge precisely how it is done. A client's trust in the confidentiality of his arrangements with a dealer is an essential factor of doing business at the upper end of the antiques trade.

Another rule of conduct is: 'Dealers unite!' It is understood that a group of acquaintances in the trade can rely on each other to support the cause when challenged by an outsider: client, taxman, auctioneer, or whoever. Relationships in the trade are constructed on the belief that dealers will all prosper or all fall together. Truly independent advice in the art market is thus very difficult to come by, as everyone has a vested interest in maintaining confidence by supporting the attributions of other dealers, right or wrong. The honest man among them can only stay loyal to his colleagues in the trade by withholding the truth rather than telling a lie. If asked his opinion by an influential client on the advisability of buying a notorious 'marriage' of two bureau bookcases in a neighbour's Bond Street premises, the honest dealer is not morally obliged to laugh in scorn and denounce the bare-faced effrontery of his rival; he can say instead, with the confidential squeeze of an elbow, 'Yes, it's quite nice, isn't it. But, you know, I've got a really superb piece in the pipeline. Absolutely original condition, too. And this one, you see, has been a little over-restored.' On this principle, if a client's insurers insist on an independent valuation of a recent group of purchases which were far from bargains and the dealer is afraid they might be valued below his selling price, the best person to recommend is his chief rival. It is, after all, very much in the rival's interests to value the kind of things he sells as expensively as possible, and few dealers would be foolish enough to execute such a valuation without a discreet telephone call to the man they know to have supplied the goods. There is seldom any problem for a good specialist in identifying the main source of supply to a collector; if he has not previously met the collector himself, he will certainly have met most of the works on their way through the trade.

The code of behaviour also insists that it is unwise to approach directly a client who is primarily handled by another dealer. Most other retail businesses try to increase their market share by stealing key clients from their rivals, but antique dealing depends so much on personal relationships and on the building up of trust in an untrustworthy world that the most successful way of selling to another dealer's client is through the dealer himself, not behind his back. Unwritten agreements grow up that a particular dealer has territorial claim over certain clients and therefore has a right to handle all their business and earn his commission. Any attempt to cross this convention would be an invitation to open warfare – antique dealers reckon that peace brings greater prosperity.

Dealers are not expected to reveal the sources of their discoveries to other members of the trade, nor to pass on the names of their favourite restorers or framers, nor to share any of the other background details which it takes years of trial and error to fill in correctly. It is accepted that this ancillary expertise must be learnt through experience, just as knowledge of the works of art themselves is acquired. Short cuts are frowned upon and the trade is innately suspicious of the young man who climbs too fast into a Mayfair seat of power.

Although many dealers are less than scrupulous in informing the public about restoration to stock, a friend in the trade would expect to be told exactly what had been done to an object he is thinking of buying. On the other hand no self-respecting trader would return a purchase to another dealer should he discover that it is not quite what it purported to be – he does not share his profits with the seller and does not expect to recoup his losses from him either. 'Buyer Beware' is the bottom-line rule in the trade for dealer and collector alike when all attempts at a compromise solution have failed.

Though individual insider-deals may be very complex in their details, the basic tenets of the trade are simple and expedient – antiques are a luxury, not a necessity, and every dealer is free to sell as much as he can, as expensively as he can, by whatever means he chooses. Dealers who do business together on a regular basis find it convenient to operate within a particular code of behaviour which has grown up over the years. Those who break this code or prefer a maverick existence of isolated independence risk competitive abuse, but insider-dealers will continue to buy from and sell to them if the profits are right. The good opinion of other dealers is not an essential prerequisite to successful trading, as several London dealers prove by running large, profitable premises despite the fact that no one in the trade ever has a polite word to say about them.

It is difficult for the public to know how they should react to the self-protective web of intrigue which surrounds the antiques trade. By playing the game and aligning himself with a clever insider-dealer, a private collector can benefit considerably in the coverage of works of art made available to him through the network. The fanatical collector values very highly the fact that he is top of the list of potential buyers to be offered an interesting item which appears anywhere on the market. If the collector is rich enough, the number of profits which are made out of him matters less than might be imagined; what he cares about most is the possession of the object ahead of rival collectors. More annoying to the collector are those shops from which the public are in effect excluded by coded price tags and the

unwillingness of the staff to give any information at all about the pieces themselves.

It might prove helpful for the public to know how these price codes are formed. All the codes are different but they are normally based on straightforward letter-for-number substitutions keyed into a remembered phrase using ten different letters, such as 'GRIM BEAUTY' where G is one, R is two, all the way to Y which is zero. The labels on objects usually have two coded numbers on them, one for the buying price and one for the minimum selling price. Code-breakers have a distinct advantage in the bargaining battle – for example if IUY/RTE is written on a label it is interesting to know that the piece cost the dealer £296 and that his minimum selling price is £380, especially if the shop assistant asks £600.

The gain to the public in buying from an independent dealer is that he may actually do more selling to private individuals than to the trade and may therefore be more generous in his bargaining with collectors. It would be unrealistic to expect those uncooperative 'Trade Only' dealers with code-priced stock to give a healthy discount to anyone not buying large quantities from them on a regular basis. The biggest discounts are given to the people on whom a particular business depends, whether they be trade or private. 'What is your best trade price?' is an overworked phrase which often does more harm than good.

The nature of the trade, with its easy money during boom times, the means it offers for taxation and currency fiddles, and its reliance on personal opinion rather than proven fact, attracts buccaneers as well as aesthetes. Insider-dealers are a law unto themselves. Much business is conducted by verbal contract and in the exchange of black cash without stock entries or recorded sales. But the freedom the trade offers to rogues is also offered to the creative dealers who enjoy the opportunity of earning a living in an individual way of their own choosing and who give much pleasure to others in so doing. No one is obliged to follow fashion and spend his or her earnings or capital on 'antiques'. Collectors have the freedom to buy where they wish or not to buy at all, just as dealers are free to sell to other dealers or to members of the public. Dealers find the clients they deserve, clients the dealers they deserve. Rights and wrongs in the trade there may be, good and bad buys there certainly are, but sorting out the right dealer from the wrong dealer, the good bronze from the bad bronze, is a matter of personal choice, of individual preference – not of moral obligation.

Three

Dealers
and
the Public

Public interest and involvement in antiques have increased enormously at all levels of the trade over the last ten years. Increased demand means increased prices, and the rapid expansion of the market in the 1960s, due principally to export demand, was sustained through the 1970s by the ever-widening fashion for collecting in Britain as well as abroad. Growing competition for the middle range of medium-priced antiques ensures that prices climb steadily upwards and the public is provided with built-in protection against the duplicity of the market place. With some notable exceptions, collectors have more often made money than lost it when disposing of their purchases in recent years. Art market pundits with a personal interest in attracting more and more investment into the field can quantify their claim that buying antiques brings pleasure with profit. It is fashion and profit which disguise the fact that the trade is full of over-valued, over-restored and over-the-top objects on which an unnecessary number of dealers make an unjustifiable amount of money. When the bubble bursts, as it has in the past and will in the future, the collectors who suffer least will be the ones that took the trouble to search out the greatest rarity on the market, the really fine dealer.

The basic qualifications which a serious collector looks for in a dealer are integrity and expertise, one of these qualities being useless without the other. There are plenty of amiable people in the trade who believe it to be true when they assure a potential customer that a Carlton House desk is Georgian or that a Ralph Wood squirrel is unrestored; the solicitor's wife in her shop in Hungerford and the golf club committee member in his showrooms in Harrogate do not intend to deceive, they simply do not know enough to realize that they are wrong. There are, on the other hand, those dealers who know a great deal about their subjects but are unable to resist the temptation of using their expertise to pass off inferior examples at inflated prices. The integrity of a dealer comes into play in the pricing of works of art as well as in their attribution. Those brazen fellows who justly pride themselves on the quality and rarity of their stock but insist on selling at double the current value are also to be avoided by the circumspect collector. The good dealer is rare but he does exist and is worth searching for. He may be found anywhere from Bond Street to the Portobello Road, and whether he sells Ming porcelain or cigarette cards, each item of stock will have been bought for a particular reason, the information supplied will be accurate and interesting, and the price will be fair.

The advantages to members of the public in buying regularly from a good dealer are numerous. The attributions are guaranteed for their authenticity and money refunded without argument should educated doubts be raised. Good dealers will also be anxious to buy back their stock when collectors wish to sell; if, for financial or other reasons, a dealer is unable to produce the money himself he would normally take back stock on consignment and find buyers from among his other customers, charging a commission of no more than 15 per cent. As fine works of art in all fields are siphoned off into museums and permanent private collections, it is commercially advantageous to have an opportunity of reacquiring stock. The combination of increasing rarity, fashionable demand, and inflationary economics can lead to an honest dealer's being able to offer a client two or three times the purchase price within a couple of years.

Other services supplied include bidding at auction without charging commission, organizing restoration, framing, storage, etc., advising on insurance and security, and hunting for specific objects to fill the gaps in a client's collection. It is a process which relies on mutual trust and brings equal benefit to both parties. The relationship between dealer and collector becomes mutually rewarding on a level beyond the merely commercial when, as often happens, clients become friends. The dealer then becomes such a frequent visitor to the collector's home that it is as if the collection, which was principally formed from his stock, remains partly his. Evenings are spent discussing the finer points of scholarship and aesthetics, assessing the worth of new publications on the subject, and reinterpreting opinions in the light of newly discovered comparative objects. The dealer keeps the collector informed of interesting items appearing elsewhere on the market and the collector informs the dealer of items he finds that are superfluous to the collection but would be useful for stock. A situation can develop where little money ever changes hands as the collector builds up credit through introducing new clients to his friend's business and purchases are paid for by the combination of this credit and the part-exchange of objects discarded from the collection in the process of upgrading. Such relationships are the most significant human contacts in the lives of those dealers and collectors alike whose only real and lasting love is for the works of art that they themselves handle.

Not many members of the public, however, wish to take the buying of antiques quite as seriously as this, and for them the important thing to remember is that the honest ignoramus is far more dangerous than the dishonest expert. The expert may be able to fool the client with restorations but the ignoramus may himself be fooled by the out-and-out fake – better to buy a restored ivory original than a perfect plastic copy. There are other useful tips for the occasional adventurer into the antiques trade. It is important to learn some of the trade jargon in order to deceive the dealers into thinking you know more than you do. The adjectives 'right' and 'wrong' carry great weight when delivered with conviction. On inspecting an oak dresser in one of those respectable West Country centres, you can do no harm by saying quietly to your companion, 'It could be a marriage. The top is absolutely right, but the mounts on the base seem wrong to me.' All oak dressers are open to criticism and the dealer will be impressed even if it happens to be the finest example he has ever owned. 'Period' is another useful word for it allows you to admire the age of a piece of furniture without knowing exactly when it was made – 'Such a wonderful patina, it must be period, don't you think?'

There are certain phrases which dealers themselves use so unthinkingly that if a member of the public slips them casually into the conversation most dealers will automatically assume that they are talking to a fellow trader – 'charmingly petite' (a small chair), 'Is it soft paste?' (a porcelain figure), 'more lead than silver' (a repaired teapot), 'It's a bit thin, has it been relined?' (an oil painting), 'great piece of gros point' (a needlework panel), 'with dovetails and dowling pins of that quality it must be English' (a chest of drawers), 'marvelous transitional parquetry on that commode' (another chest of drawers).

Reduced prices and honest background information can result from the assumption that a trade deal is being done. Actions can be deceptive too, and amateurs might care to practise at home some of the standard professional skills of the trade. The drawers of sideboards must be opened with the appropriate movement of head and neck; side-chairs are picked up with a deft flick and a glancing inspection given underneath; a coin can be passed around the rim of a jardinière, tapped on the hand of a Columbine figure, and placed on the front of a pier glass; and the most difficult trick of them all is to lick and bite the spout of a Chelsea cream jug, then nod knowingly.

More straightforwardly, it is sensible to ask for a detailed invoice ascribing date, material and country of origin to the object being purchased. The buyer is well protected by the Trades Description Acts and the Sale of Goods Acts if he can produce a detailed, receipted invoice which is signed and titled by the dealer. Once a price is agreed, the dealer will appreciate the immediate payment and clearance of the purchase – many dealers favour prompt payers with a discount next time they buy. Never believe a dealer who tells you what an article cost him in an attempt to prove how little money he is making. Seldom are dealers to be trusted who reduce their asking prices massively to a casual passerby. Remember that, as in life at large, the most charming dealers are often the most dangerous and beware of the grey-haired tweed-jacketed cigarillo smoker with roving watery eyes who does not appear to be trying to sell you anything at all.

More specific advice on how the general public might best approach the trade as buyers can be given by discussing the

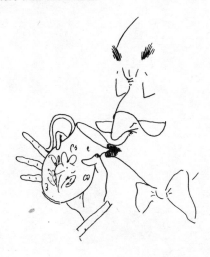

various different types of dealer and their clients, beginning, as in the first chapter, with the West End Emporiums.

For all practical purposes the Emporiums are reserved for no more than two kinds of client, the rich and the very rich. The richer a person is, or purports to be, the better the service supplied; and the merest hint of an empty penthouse overlooking Hyde Park will bring a rush of blood to the head of the urbane shopkeeper and a reduction in price for an initial purchase in the hopes of many more to follow. With most of the stock priced in tens of thousands, a flourishing reduction of 30 per cent from £1,000 to £700 on some nicknack for a guest bedroom is no more than bait to catch the masterpiece for the drawing-room at £80,000. In selling to the very rich, an experienced dealer realizes that the cost itself does not really matter and the reduction in price is no more than a gesture indicating the dealer's

willingness to provide satisfaction in matters of greater concern.

The matter of greatest concern to the clients of the West End Emporiums is the acquisition of works of art which will be recognized by others as of the highest quality. The unadventurous taste of the newly rich is explained by this need for recognition, and it is the dealer's job to supply a show of culture which will be instantly and uncritically admired. The reputation of the dealer, the pedigree of the previous owner and the expense of the purchase are all

things which breed confidence in an area where many
people are so unsure of themselves. For many of the
Emporium's clients it is not the beauty of the object itself
which brings pleasure, but the feeling of being able to relax
in its presence knowing that it is telling their friends that
they have both money and taste.

In this environment the invoice is almost as important as
the object, and the creation of a rare invoice is a fine art in its
own right. The hand-made paper is either very thick or very
thin, and the tasteful letterhead implies by its engraved

design a company origin dating back into the eighteenth century. The ultimate guarantee of satisfaction for the uncertain buyer comes in finding from the invoice that the firm actually is older than the antique; extra comfort is derived from the majority of directors having the same surname as the firm itself. Then to the description – the most impressive way a descriptive invoice can begin is with a capitalized title such as 'The Wappingham Violoncello' or 'The Von Asbach Garniture', the implication being that the violoncello or garniture is so famous that further description is superfluous, a fact which should not deter the dealer from supplying a minimum five-line eulogy stuffed with all the esoteric technical words which the new owner will learn to drop at opportune moments. The names of the craftsman and designers must then be listed with their dates and passing reference acknowledged of other works of art made by them now in various national museums, and perhaps direct comparison proposed with something more or less similar 'in the possession of Her Majesty the Queen'. The provenance is most impressive when very short, as in 'Commissioned by Baron Ferdinand von Asbach in January 1722 and thence by direct descent', but if not short it must be very long, listing numerous occasions of admired public exhibition, references to learned dissertations on the object, the proof of its having passed over the years from one famous collection to another. A photograph of the original design or of the piece in pride of place in some magnificent Victorian setting warms the hearts of the insecure. And at the end of the invoice, the price. This must be large enough to be taken seriously but not so large as that of a Picasso. The cost of a Picasso is the standard price of purchasing kudos; kudos at anything less is in some way a bargain, and gives the client a sense of having made money, not spent it.

The directors of the Emporiums understand their clients, for most of them are equally rich in possessions and equally conservative in taste. The Rolls-Royce parked on the double yellow lines outside Kimberley's is just as likely to belong to the eldest Mr Kimberley as to one of the family's clients. Between old Mr Kimberley's friends at the Carlton Club and young Mr Kimberley's wife's relations, the firm is in contact with a large number of people who might be attracted by the idea of the secret sale of a family heirloom for funds abroad. The Kimberleys themselves and most of their clients own 'back-to-back' companies in the Dutch Antilles, numbered accounts on Lac Léman, and turbo-foil 'yachts' in Monte Carlo harbour, so the putting together of tax-free deals for buyer and seller is standard practice. If the Kimberleys and their like were not totally at ease with the vast sums of money involved at the upper end of the antiques business, they would be unable to do either the buying or the selling.

No one knows better than the rich that you get no more than you pay for, sometimes less. It is perfectly obvious that a great deal of money is spent by the Emporiums on decor and presentation, and that these expenses, all the other overheads and the considerable salaries of the directors are all added to the price of the stock. Though knowing the truth, people purchasing such luxuries like to live under the illusion that they are getting at least something for nothing. The something that they expect for nothing is all the trimmings – immaculate packing, free delivery at the pre-cisely convenient moment (preferably by liveried porters), espresso coffee or herbal tea and flattering chatter whenever they are in the West End with time (theirs) to spare, interest-free credit for up to three months, the efficient supervision of collection and restoration of bibelots bought from un-known shops in Bloomsbury, and the procurement of places for their offspring at Harrow and Eton followed by courses at Christie's and Sotheby's. The dealer knows the game and simply remembers to add a few thousand pounds to the price he quotes on their next purchase if he has not already done so on the last – or even if he has, why not do so again, for prices at this level of the trade are arbitrary.

Prices at the large general specialists have a more discernible structure, and members of the public would be well advised to look around carefully before making any commitments. To anyone but the experienced collector, the large specialists all look much the same at first sight and the only way of choosing among them might appear to be simply by whichever has the right sized table at an affordable price. This would be to make a fundamental mistake in the method of approaching the traditional-taste stock handled by the large general specialists in London – patience is the necessary virtue, patience to wait not just for any Georgian mahogany dining table to seat ten, but for a particularly unusual one which will bring increasing rather than passing satisfaction. Interestingly, the slightly quirky, far rarer example sometimes costs less than the standard type simply because it is different and therefore not instantly recognizable as good taste by the fashion-conscious public. This is an area where the collector who does research into his subject and into the market place will be rewarded.

As many of the private buyers in this 'establishment' part of the antiques trade lead busy commercial lives of their own, it is impossible for them to spend more than a stolen hour or two a week chasing around town after bargains. The research therefore has to be done largely at weekends and in the evenings, and the busy collector keeps in touch with what is going on through detailed inspection of auction catalogues, specialist magazines and all related publications.

Since much of the stock at the large London specialists is bought at auction, subscription to the relevant London auctions and to the main provincial sales allows the collector to keep pace with market developments. Careful perusal of the advertisements in magazines like *Connoisseur* and *Apollo* gives a general idea of who is selling what, and evening previews of exhibitions in museums and of the important trade fairs provide further information. Dealers are always impressed by the hard-working banker who manages to keep informed of exactly what is going on in the trade. Rather than compete with the dealers at auction, the busy banker would prefer to reserve an interesting chair, engraved wine glass or whatever over the telephone immediately after the sale and then take his time before deciding whether to buy it or not. And, of course, the collector who does his homework often knows what the dealer paid and can be tougher in bargaining.

There are other points worth remembering. Dealers in these traditional fields tend to be cautious in their conduct of business and attach considerable significance to speedy turnover. They would, by and large, be happy to take £3,000 for a set of chairs within a week of purchasing them, even if certain unusual features might suggest that £4,000 could be secured if they waited a bit. The collector who wishes to buy these more interesting examples must make sure that his favourite dealers know of his particular interests and that they contact him when such things turn up. The only way of insuring this is by keeping in constant contact and responding immediately to any messages. It is no use asking for photographs, delaying the decision for weeks on end, and then saying no, for the dealer will never bother to telephone again. Most dealers will turn up at their shops before breakfast if necessary to show a client new stock, and would prefer an immediate negative decision to an indefinite reservation. Members of the public naively ask dealers how they can bear parting with all their beautiful stock – the obvious answer to this is that the pleasure of selling at a profit far outweighs the sadness of losing a fine object, and anyway the sanguine dealer reckons that there is always something else interesting to go out and buy, and to sell again. Many of the best dealers find satisfaction in the chase not in the possession, and in the placing of an object in the right collection at a pleasing profit. Do not be duped by those hypocritical dealers who protest concern only for art, not for commerce – antique dealers are no different from high-street traders in cuddly toys, the job of both is to market as much merchandise as possible. Pin-striped suits, plums in the mouth, and posh premises do not transform a trader into an aesthete.

With the narrow specialists, members of the public have a far better chance of forming relationships in which the commercial basis of the contact need not colour the growth of friendship. Much depends on the individual collector and dealer, and on the subject of specialization; there can be no rules or formulas, but there is greater potential for personal discovery and fulfilment in this area of the antiques trade than in any other.

The binding agent between the narrow specialists and their customers is not knowledge itself but the thirst for it. Offer the specialist a sign that, however inexpert and uninformed you may be, there is natural enthusiasm for and genuine interest in the subject, and the doors of locked cupboards will be thrown open and the way ahead mapped out for a lifetime of enjoyable collecting. A sympathetic dealer feels little respect for the client who buys six fine works of art in a ten-minutes gallop around the shop without even bothering to find out exactly why they are what the dealer proudly describes them as being. It brings in the money and the business will not be turned away, but the dealer's personal interest is aroused by the couple visiting his shop for the first time who spend half an hour or so quietly inspecting every piece and then buy one cheap but unusual item. The dealer suspects that if the couple return they will have some intelligent questions to ask about their exploratory purchase and will probably decide to buy another piece which they had been eyeing on their first visit. From these beginnings the great collections develop.

How, the inexperienced collector would be justified in asking, does one find a reliable specialist in an affordable field? The object is first to find the field before worrying about which dealer, and it needs to be a field which provokes a natural response but is not so much in fashion that the cost of the best pieces exceeds most people's yearly income. The only way to do this is to read and to look – read as many books on the decorative arts as one can buy or borrow, and look at as many dealers' shops and auction rooms as one can manage. From the wide choice on offer, narrow the options down to those subjects which appear to have intrinsic quality, to be readily available, and which, most importantly, have a personal appeal. Then it is back to the books to learn as much as one can about the final short-list of subjects (the library of the Victoria and Albert Museum, open to everyone during gallery opening hours, is an excellent place to study) and finally a sortie around the trade to identify the best specialists in these fields. Armed with the basic knowledge and an inquisitive mind, one can tell relatively easily whether a dealer is a genuine expert or not. An evasive answer to direct questions on technique is one sign of ailing expertise; so is the sing-song production of glib patter, and a dealer's need to consult his own labels before remembering details of date and attribution. If a decent specialist seems impossible to find after looking around shops and markets in the various antiques enclaves in London, then enquiries should be made among the more friendly general dealers and as often as not the same name will be recommended time and again for a particular field. As to judgment on price and value, this can only come with experience and it is best to build this experience by buying at the cheaper end of the market to begin with. The price a collector pays for an object, and whether he considers it to be good or bad value, depends so much on the importance of the object in relation to the rest of his collection that there can be no ultimate ruling. The good dealer will have a fair idea how much the market will stand for a particular piece and the honest dealer will not want to ask any more than this; in the final analysis only the buyer can decide how much something is worth, and indeed it actually is worth at that moment no more and no less than a collector decides to pay for it.

The most creative and exciting thing a collector can do in the antiques market is to find a field about which little has been written in recent times and capture the subject for his own private amusement. Even better if the chosen field is positively vilified by fashionable opinion despite the fact that at its time of manufacture and among previous collecting generations it was highly prized. As antiques have already passed the test of time, collecting them is normally a safe and unimaginative exercise of established taste, and it is only in unrecognized fields that collecting becomes a challenging question of personal judgment. It involves almost as much self-confidence and critical ability as collecting the work of unknown living artists and craftsmen, and the

amateur can quite easily beat the professionals. It is amazing
how much information the dedicated, not to say fanatical,
collector can amass about a subject on which the research
files of the leading auction houses are empty. However
narrow a dealer's specialist subject and however knowledgeable he may be, there are always private collectors who
know more than he does about aspects of his subject. These
amateur experts are not always grey-bearded Mephis-
topheles, and listening to a young enthusiast spilling out
information about Cotswold craftsmen or high-fired glazing
is one of the irresistible pleasures of the trade – that is, to
any dealer interested in people as well as in objects.

The point about specialization is that it attracts people,
either as dealers or collectors, who are interested in making
some personal statement through the works of art they
handle. The motivation for entering an unrecognized field is
never kudos and is seldom investment, though the potential
for capital appreciation is considerable. Companionship can
be a motive, the desire to become part of a small group of
enthusiasts who share in and protect their exclusive little
world. The desire to form a collection which will one day be
appreciated for its international stature is certainly the aim
of some, particularly the creatively inclined who may doubt
their ability to express themselves in direct artistic terms and
therefore choose the medium of appreciation and selection
as their quasi-art. For others, devotion to an esoteric field of
collecting is a means of escape from the harshness of the
world in which they work into the cocoon of collecting in
which they play. The dealer necessarily has a more worldly
attitude to his subject than the collectors, but he appreciates
their needs and characters, indeed he earns his living by
nourishing their foibles. There are many ways in which the
specialist gives a unique service to his most serious collec-

tors. The searching-out of an unrecorded rarity to complement a client's collection has been mentioned before – such
a discovery would be hidden away out of sight at the back of
the shop so that rival collectors do not spot it before the
favoured client has had time to call in. Rare reference works,
already present in the dealer's library, may appear as
Christmas gifts to a collector friend. An expensive addition
to the collection can be taken home for a month's trial free of
all charges and obligations. And the pleasure given by a
specialist dealer to one of his collector friends is often
unconnected with the actual acquisition of works of art –
bringing two collectors into social contact is of immeasurable
benefit in personal terms; the introduction of collectors to
museum curators for the arrangement of loans to special
exhibitions also brings great satisfaction to the proud
owners; and there is the advice about places of interest to
visit, lectures to attend, related subjects to think about,
societies to join, and other aspects of living that a sensitive
dealer likes to see being enjoyed by his clients.

The job of the dealer-decorators is also to serve the public
more directly than in many other areas of the trade. There,
however, similarity with the narrow specialists ends, for the
decorators swim with the tide of fashion, not against it, and
their clients are seeking the approval of their idols instead of
the companionship of their peers. Totally different criteria
come into play.

Whatever they may claim to the contrary, clients go to
dealer-decorators for one reason only, to insure that the
decor and contents of their homes are as comfortably
fashionable as can be. Since the antiques supplied by
decorators are charged at a premium and the clients are also
paying vast sums for new carpets, curtains, upholstery, and
probably new doors, ceiling mouldings, bathrooms and

chimney-pieces, they might as well go for the best while they are about it. 'The best' means a dealer-decorator who knows a good deal about period architecture as well as modern fashion and who makes sure that all the works of art he supplies are absolutely genuine. And as clients who need a dealer-decorator in the first place presumably lack either the confidence or the imagination (or both) to make their own choice of colours and styles, it is also worth commissioning one of the decorators who has a sense of fun and extravagance, not any of those conservative purveyors of regency stripes for the sofas, rose-trailed lattice-work wallpaper for the bedrooms, and Sheraton satinwood furniture for the dining-room. There is safe fashion and splendid fashion; both are expensive, so at least enjoy the benefits of wealth and encourage a well-known decorator to create something original and amusing. Great decorators can even make it seem personal as well.

Decorator-dealers rely on the same kind of clients who go to the dealer-decorators, except that their customers make a show of independence in so far as they choose their antiques and bric-a-brac for themselves instead of leaving it to the decorator. Not that the choice is so very wide, for the style and the range are dictated by fashion – successful buyers must be expert in matters of fashion and be able to recognize works of art which are thought to be good without necessarily knowing anything about them. It is the effect which matters, not the facts; it makes no difference that the Berlin woolwork on the shellback of the Victorian nursing chair began life as a fire-screen, or that the chair's legs were taken from a sideboard. It would not really matter if the upholstered chair was totally new, provided that it copied an original model and the material was old. In many cases the dealers themselves do not pretend to know much about what they are selling either; indeed there is no reason why they should feel obliged to, so long as they are not presenting their stock as anything more than high-priced fashion. Entertaining shops stuffed with odd relics of the past to which respect is paid, not because they are old, but because they are attractive and saleable, are more admirable in many ways than those precious antique shops tastefully laid out with fine works of art to which the staff refer in hushed voices of admiration.

Real collectors would be unwise to turn their noses up at the decorator-dealers, for rarities often lurk among the stock destined for the decorators themselves and for foreign shippers. The prices on the labels are always intentionally high, so as to enable decorators to bring in their clients without being embarrassed about their own price structure. Hence this is one shop where it is well worth bargaining, and the best way of approaching the decorator-dealer is to explain that you are indeed a private collector and would like to make a particular purchase if the price could possibly be brought down to a more realistic level. The chances are that 30 per cent or so will be knocked off the marked price and the collector will walk out of the shop with a rarity which would have cost three times as much at a specialist's.

The private dealer can be a daunting figure for a member of the general public to address through the intercom of a triple-locked door on the upper floors of Bond Street premises. The wares and the customers, it is implied, are exclusive. As such private dealers hold a small range of stock generally at high prices, the deals are infrequent and unhurried. In places like this the client is not simply allowed to ask for all the information it is possible to know about an intended purchase, he is expected to insist on such a service. With the best private dealers it is a matter of pride to supply a more detailed analysis of a work of art than is available in any reference book; indeed they are unlikely to offer an object for sale until they have unearthed some original piece of research and been able to prove a positive attribution to a significant artist. This, after all, is what the collector is paying for, total security in the quality, condition, originality and historical importance of his expensive investment. This is one of the few areas of the trade where the previous source of supply is willingly revealed to the buyer, even if the private dealer has bought the object recently at public auction for a tenth of the price he is asking – the embarrassment is not the dealer's but the auctioneer's for not doing his research well enough and the Bond Street rivals' for failing to spot a pearl among the swine.

The other characteristic feature of the conduct of business in the private dealer's velvet-lined lair is complete confidentiality. No one need ever know who has bought what, how and where it was paid for, when and by whom it was collected, or to which location it was taken. Secret practices suit the dealer as much as the client, for a relatively modest turnover and commensurate life-style as acknowledged to the British tax man can easily conceal a trans-Continental panoply of wealth. One of the principal reasons for using this kind of up-market private dealer instead of the equally up-market Emporium or specialist shop is the matter of secrecy. It is surprising how many wealthy collectors are obsessively secret about purchasing works of art; men who lead flamboyant social and business lives angrily insist that there should be no written record of their art market transactions, and the discreet private dealer is about the only person in the trade who can guarantee to preserve the anonymity of his clients. While auction houses sometimes attempt to hide the identify of their buyers and sellers, their organizations are too large to prevent leakages, and anyway the government regularly makes use of its right of inspection of the company books. Thus private dealers are frequently entrusted with elephantine commission bids when some great rarity at auction forces the secrétive collector to compete in the public arena. He far prefers, however, to make his purchases behind electronically closed doors where the private dealer and he sit alone with a magnificent rarity consigned secretly to the dealer by an aristocratic owner who will never be told the name of the new owner of his family heirloom.

Not all private dealers wish to live on the breathless summits of the art market. Some modest individuals sell from their own homes rather than smart premises in order to avoid this rarefied life and because they like to choose with whom they do business, and when. It is difficult for members of the public to locate such private dealers, indeed the contact usually comes from the other direction, the dealers ringing up a particular collector whom a friend in the trade recommends as being interested in their kind of thing. Once the contact has been made a serious collector's relationship with a good private dealer of this sort almost always blossoms into a delightful friendship, with none of the competitive pressures which inevitably surround dealers in shops accessible to the public. With minimal overheads and a more personal approach to life, private dealers also offer better value than their rivals in the public sector.

Private dealers provide their clients with many of the services which are also available from art market consultants and agents, the difference being that dealers are principally concerned with disposing of their own stock whereas consultants are exclusively involved in offering a service. Truly independent advice is a rarity in the art market, and the good agent will refuse to compromise his position by participating as a principal, by acting on a retainer from a dealer, by accepting commission from a third party or by doing anything which might prejudice the independence of his views. The only trouble is that as most agents work on commission from works of art successfully bought or sold they have a vested interest in persuading their clients to spend money in the market when, on occasions, they might be better advised not to. One way round this problem is for the client to guarantee payment of a retainer to the consultant or to pay a fee for a feasibility study, regardless of whether any transactions are made. This is particularly important in the management of portfolio investment in the art market which the independent agent is uniquely suited to handle, provided that he is offered an incentive share in the profitability of the investment and is adequately rewarded for his negative advice.

An art market consultant is not expected to know everything himself, but he is required to know who has the answers and how they can be extracted. Contacts are the tools of the consultants' trade, and all of them will be able to drop the right names – the question is whether the 'names' have ever heard of the consultant and, if so, whether they have any respect for him. A prospective client would be well advised to ask around the trade before committing himself to a particular agent or consultant, for they tend to be people who have moved from some other part of the trade, not always for the best of reasons, and they can all string together a convincing line of promises; as in other professions, those who offer the earth may turn out to be worms.

There are some marvellous characters in the art market who come under the category of consultant, though adviser might be a better way of describing them. They are those eccentric scholars and itinerant writers on the decorative arts and architecture who find themselves in the enviable position of being confidante, chief guru, chauffeur, and, in effect, sole agent to wealthy collectors of distinction. It is a position that every art market consultant would give his gold-capped eye-teeth for, but it goes to those who not only have a naturally non-commercial approach to life but who are also extremely generous with whatever money should happen to come their way. The rich man is happy to reward such advisers with his trust because he knows that their pleasure is taken from the works of art themselves and not from the money needed to acquire them. Part-time advisers of this nature have been, and are still, behind many of the finest collections formed in Great Britain.

'Trade Only' dealers are what they announce themselves to be, reserved for the trade and therefore of no direct concern to the general public. Some of the big warehouse dealers whose main business is in wholesale containerized export to all parts of the world do, however, welcome private buyers, so long as they pay on the nail and take whatever they see without wishing to know what it is and where it came from. This attitude is born not of a desire to conceal but from lack of interest; as far as the wholesalers are concerned, their business is in 'brown furniture', 'smalls', 'shipping goods', 'household effects' and the rest, and they are not bothered about the age and origins of the lorry-loads of materials passing through their hands so long as there is a profit. Since the requirements of the foreign clients tend to be fairly standardized, the wholesalers buy in a safe and uninteresting sort of way, but occasionally unusual things can be found in their warehouses; when buying a job lot at auction or in doing a house clearance, they sometimes end up with things they do not really want but which are too cheap to resist. Needless to say, when the esoteric rarity is discovered among the stacks and shelves of ordinary 'antiques', it can often be bought for very little. It is also always worth offering to pay cash in return for a discount on the price, though only a collector with the nerve of a souk Arab insists on bargaining on a bargain. A visit to one of the wholesale warehouses is also a good idea for a member of the public who is anxious to furnish a house quickly with more or less antique furniture and decorative objects. The selection is much wider than at any of the secondary salerooms and the prices are usually reasonable, as it is a low mark-up, quick turnover business. No need to ring up before and ask the wholesaler if he has a pedestal desk in at the moment; the answer, if not an expletive, will be, 'How many do you want?'

The small general dealers in shops, arcades, and antiques markets are so varied in character and quality (as indeed are their clients) that it is impossible to give detailed practical advice. Most people who frequent this area of the trade do so out of curiosity, not through any driving collecting passion, and the rules are straightforward enough, if not cliché: buy only what you like at prices you can afford. The more regularly and carefully people look around small general dealers' all over London, the easier it will become to buy cheaply; but as prices tend to catch up with themselves it is a pity to leave behind something which is exactly the right size and style just because it seems slightly overpriced. Provided that the out-and-out fakes are avoided, the down-side risks are never too high, as at least some of one's money can be recovered at short notice through the auctions – and there is always the chance of a profit.

The serious collector, unless he has a great deal of spare time, keeps in regular contact with the select number of small general dealers who understand his field of interest, and forgets about the rest of them. Small dealers can be extremely useful to a collector for, lacking the knowledge and confidence to buy aggressively in esoteric fields, they are more willing to make purchases on commission than is the specialist who prefers to buy on his own account and sell on to the collector at a profit, the larger the better. Once a good relationship is built up, the small dealer telephones the collector whenever he sees something of potential interest in another shop or in an auction, describes it in detail, having taken note of all the marks, signatures or inscriptions and any damage, and takes instructions from there. It makes sense for the collector to reward the dealer generously when he buys a rarity on commission at a low price instead of sticking to the standard 10 or 15 per cent. However, when buying for the first time from a small general dealer, the private collector would do best to conceal his knowledge, for a covetous dash across the shop alerts the dealer to the possibility of his owning a hidden rarity, which he may then decide either is not for sale until he has checked it out with one of the leading auction houses, or is double the price he had been thinking of asking. The technique is to wander haphazardly about the shop asking inane questions about a variety of things, to hesitate over a couple of pieces, and then casually to notice the rarity. Many collectors are clever at playing the game up to this point, but finally give themselves away by inspecting the object of interest in such minute detail that the dealer realizes he is facing an expert who knows exactly what he is looking for.

Regular visits to Bermondsey before dawn on winter Fridays, and rain-soaked Saturdays in Portobello Market are exclusive to fanatics. Those collectors who seldom miss their weekly trysts with the open-market stallholders are persecuted by the fear that if one day they decided to loaf at home then the work of art for which they had been waiting all their lives would turn up at a bargain price and be bought by one of their rivals. And so it becomes a habit, an enjoyable habit shared by many dealers and not a few collectors who gossip together at their favourite snack bars and show off their discoveries, endlessly wrapping and unwrapping newspaper packages carried in plastic bags. The merits of individual snack bars also come in for a fair amount of critical analysis, it being generally agreed that the ideal would be the speedy service of a choice of fresh filter coffee; fried egg, bacon, sausage and mushrooms on hot plates; toasted ham and cheese sandwiches, doughnuts warm from the bakery; and home-made black cherry-topped cheesecake. The main exercise of the day is to call in turn on all the stallholders whom the collector has cultivated and educated over the years to root out those works of art which interest him. If the collector is a reliable weekly attendant and a regular buyer, the stallholder normally keeps things hidden to show him first. There may be quite a crowd round the stall but a regular calling out from the back of the queue, 'Anything for me this week, Ted?' will be handed over the hidden possibles for inspection. Often the piece of porcelain or silver, or whatever, is not exactly what the collector is looking for but as long as the price is acceptable he likes to buy anything the dealer is particularly pleased to have found, in order to encourage him to keep on looking. The experienced collector realizes that, here at the lower end of the trade as among the Bond Street specialists, the key to the business is personal relationships, the loyalty between dealer and collector being of great value to both parties. Collectors locked out from this inner circle bitterly accuse dealers of treating their favourites to all the best things at lower prices than they would ask anyone else. In a sense, this is true but it is not a question of favouritism; it is a sensible and enjoyable way of doing business, for the collectors have earned their privileges by spending a great deal of money over the years with the dealers who give them special treatment.

'Runners', those dealers who hawk their stock from shop to shop in battered station-wagons piled high with seeming junk, seldom come into contact with the general public. Any collector fortunate enough to make the acquaintance of a good runner should send a silent prayer of gratitude up to heaven and slip quietly under the chain of insider-dealing.

It is well known by now, courtesy of Roald Dahl and others, that 'knockers' should be cursed whereas 'runners' may be praised. The trouble is that some runners obtain their goods by knocking, literally calling at people's doors to ask if they have any antiques to sell. The practice is thought to have been most prominent in Ireland where the technique was to offer an inordinate amount of money for the first object seen through the half-open door in the hope of picking up for nothing some marvellous coup in the sitting-room. Knockers were far more active in the 1960s than they are now, for the publicity given to record auction sales has alerted the public to the possible value of almost anything. Indeed the pendulum has swung the other way and too many people now delude themselves into thinking that their trash is treasure. The temptation to accept cash on the doorstep for a bashed bit of pottery must be considerable, but the wearying perseverance of the knockers once they have made a single purchase usually leads to trouble. Anyway, it is a palpably fraudulent way of earning a living and knockers should be resisted on all occasions if not actually reported to the authorities.

As buyers, museums are in a sense acting for the public at large, but their buying is done from a very narrow range of dealers. There are three reasons for this. First, and most pertinently, there are few dealers with sufficient expertise and academic know-how to handle museum requirements. Secondly, the whole process of museum acquisition is so laborious that many dealers who would normally be interested in doing museum business and quite frequently hold stock of museum calibre, cannot be bothered to go through the whole time-wasting process and instead sell to private collectors. Thirdly, the staffing structure does not allow for curators and their assistants to spend time in the market place discovering for their institutions – as with their expertise they undoubtedly would – those masterpieces which float around unrecognized. The effect of all this is that sales from the antiques trade to the museums take place mainly through a chosen few in traditional fields at extremely high prices.

Close personal contact with the museums is confined to the narrow specialists where shared enthusiasm and knowledge for a particular subject bring the curator and the dealer together outside the purely commercial sphere. The specialist is naturally well acquainted with the public collections in his field, and through academic journals and societies he also has personal contact with many scholars. On acquiring a little-known masterpiece, the dealer's immediate reaction is to send photographs around to the relevant museum keepers and university professors in order to canvass opinions and exchange ideas. The procedure is of mutual benefit to the museums and the dealers, for the museum man is enabled to inspect and record an important item before it is sold to a private collector, possibly abroad, and the dealer enjoys the privilege of a personal judgment from an internationally recognized authority. The value of a firm attribution to an important designer by a museum expert is considerable – it can triple the saleability of an object. Dealers can also help museums by lending rare, hidden items of stock to special exhibitions and by putting the curators in touch with little-known private collectors. Provided that their names are not given, or, in some cases, on precisely the opposite condition, collectors are honoured by the museum association, and the museums are delighted to be able to add to their records the location of another group of important works.

All this enhances the dealer's reputation with the authorities and makes it somewhat easier for him to sell things to museums should he wish to do so. As the new purchasing grants become available for use at the beginning of April each year, informed dealers make their proposals to contacts in the museums many months in advance so that all the research and paperwork can be completed for immediate consideration by the director and board of trustees. In some departments the whole annual grant is spent before the end of the first few weeks on items which dealers have been holding for many months on the private understanding that the sale would go through without opposition. This has the advantage to the museum that by pre-arrangement it secures what it wants; the disadvantage is that dealers charge considerably more in order to compensate for the money being tied up for so long. In fact, those dealers who become involved in regular business with the museums discover that the actual price really hardly matters at all; historical significance is what really counts. Clever dealers make a great deal of money by supplying their museum contacts with works of art to fill the gaps in the collections and about which enough juicy information is known to fill a large description card. Purchases that are appealing to the public and inarguably 'important' bring young assistant keepers into the directors' good favour; on the academic side of the fence a career advances, on the commercial side a bank balance increases.

Much has been said about how the public can protect themselves in the antiques market, but the approach of some collectors to the dealers is so unpleasant that they deserve to be caught by every trick of the trade. If it is dishonest to sell Victorian reproductions at high prices to people who think they are Georgian originals, then it is also dishonest to delay payment on a delivered purchase for months beyond the agreed date of settlement. The cavalier way in which some collectors insist on reserving interesting stock for weeks on end is also more than a little annoying for the dealer. As well as the money-wasters there are the time-wasters, those inconsiderate bores who bellow forth their unwanted opinions at inordinate length and disturb not just the dealer but his other customers as well. Less offensive but equally frustrating are the indecisive fussers for whom nothing can ever be right. If a piece of furniture is in excellent condition they are worried about its not looking antique enough, if it shows the passing of time then it is about to fall apart; they want to buy a pair of candlesticks but silver needs cleaning, earthenware is not fine enough, porcelain is too fragile, glass too glittery, ormolu too heavy, enamel too showy, pewter too plain, and everything too expensive anyway because it will encourage burglaries. Why, the bewildered dealer asks himself, do they bother to look, why do they upset themselves by coming in at all, knowing that they will be faced by all these insoluble problems? A decent dealer does not forget that no one is obliged to buy antiques, and secretly admires those people who prove the originality of their taste by buying everything new.

Collecting antiques is most rewarding in undiscovered areas of the decorative arts and is most enjoyable when done through knowledgeable specialists. While collectors require expertise and experience in order to avoid making mistakes in the antiques trade, there are also dangers in being oversuspicious. Really good dealers are a rarity and, having found one, the most foolish thing a collector can do is to insult his integrity by never believing a word he says.

Four

Dealers
and the
Auctioneer

In public, dealer and auctioneer play the part of boon companions, innocent chums serving the good of the community by providing works of art for its enjoyment. In private, they fight a fierce battle over the rich pickings of the London art and antiques market, the spoils of war these days being divided more or less equally between the two.

Since the beginnings of the London antiques market in the late seventeenth century, dealers and auctioneers have participated side by side in the business of selling works of art to collectors. Fundamentally they are allies with a shared interest in keeping the peace in their territory so that the volume of business can continue unimpeded its remarkable rate of increase. And they have joint enemies too, any individual or government that threatens to interfere with their exclusive market place or tries to suggest that collectors might be the victims of the system instead of the victors. On the basic issues a united front is presented, and the public remains unaware of the precise nature of the internal criticism and intense rivalry. For a short period in the late 1970s dealers and auctioneers mistakenly allowed their private feuding to become public, but the danger to stability wrought by this unseemly strife was quickly realized and they have returned to the beaming, back-slapping routine of music hall bonhomie. Regrets are expressed on both sides about disagreements concerning the buyer's premium, over which the dealers threatened to take the auctioneers to the High Court; the situation has not changed one bit, but the leading West End dealers and auctioneers seem to have come to a private undersanding about their most pressing problems. As in so many other situations, illusions are carefully presented to the public and reality kept under cover.

Behind the scenes the battle still rages as the dealers try to regain some of the ground they have lost over the last twenty years. Before the Second World War it was the dealers who could afford to run offices in London, Paris and New York and the auctioneers who stayed at home; but with an unbeatable combination of charm, ruthlessness, expertise, and adventurousness the leading London auctioneers took control of the international market during the 1960s. Few dealers would argue with the assertion that it was an auctioneer, not a dealer, who contributed most tellingly to the transformation of the art market from a cosy coterie of collectors into the flashbulb-popping, record-shattering jamboree that it is today. In the past it was the great dealers about whom books were written and whose names were in the headlines; now it is the auctioneers. Dealers have become more fashionable but less powerful. Yet the potential for change in the backstage hierarchy still exists, and dealers can comfort themselves with the knowledge that the prize is far more valuable now, should they succeed in winning it back; anyway, while they may have lost to the auction houses their controlling share in the art market, the slice they currently gobble is very much larger than the whole pre-war cake. It is the convention to complain, but everyone at the upper end of the art market is doing so well that the last thing they want is to upset confidence by fighting in public over fakes, rings, guarantees, commissions, or anything else. Neither dealer nor auctioneer wants fashionable clientele to be frightened off through doubts about the expertise and integrity of either side of the trade. Dealers and auctioneers share the same nightmare, that a craze for collecting orchids and animals might sweep the Western world, banishing 'antiques' to charity stalls and forgotten attics. All nightmares have a factual basis – a hundred years ago brand new furnishings were the fashion, and the most prosperous auctioneer in London was a gentleman called Stevens who sold botanical and zoological specimens, dead and alive, from splendid premises in Covent Garden.

From a purely commercial point of view, the auction houses are bound to keep on friendly terms with their allies in the trade because dealers, either on their own account or as agents, buy on average 80 per cent of the lots sold at auction in London and provide a sizeable percentage of the property sent in for sale as well. This leads to what is known in the City as 'a special relationship'.

As potential buyers, many dealers are favoured with auction privileges granted to few private individuals. Specialist dealers tend to be on friendly terms with the corresponding experts in the rooms and are given liberal access to the departments to look over items destined for future sales. An auctioneer does not expect a dealer to give away information about a work of art he is likely to be bidding on at auction, but if a difficult object is shown to enough specialists at least one of them will be free to give a helpful clue and an opinion as to the likely value. It is understood by both parties that such arrangements must be mutually beneficial if they are going to work, and close personal friendships often emerge from this sharing of commercial interests. Departmental experts know how helpful to the success of their sales it can be for a dealer to have inspected an important item three or four weeks before the public viewing – the dealer then has more time to hunt around for prospective clients, and is more likely to turn up at the sale with a hefty bid. Free catalogues are sent out to dealers whose competitive attendance at a sale is courted, and a respected dealer is often given helpful information not printed in the catalogue, such as the identity of the owner. Though confidential information about reserves and commission bids can only be extracted by under-the-counter bribery of a corruptible employee, it is not difficult for an experienced dealer to discover the level of competition by judicious questioning of contacts in the rooms. In bidding at auction, it is very useful to know the reserve price which has been agreed between the auctioneer and the vendor, for it is best not to bid below this figure and to let the item fail to sell, be 'bought in' or 'B.I.' as the jargon has it. After the auction the departmental head will try to persuade the owner to accept a lower offer through a private sale; otherwise he fails to earn his extra 10 per cent buyer's premium.

At the auction itself, regular dealers have their favourite seats automatically reserved for them, often at the aptly named ring, a horsehoe-shaped table covered in baize extending out into the room below the auctioneer's rostrum. Dealers known to the auctioneer are sometimes given what is called 'a quick hammer' (a lot is knocked down sharply without searching for other offers in order to encourage dilatory bidders to make up their minds more quickly – a practice which gives rather more satisfaction to the buyer than it does to the seller). The porters are naturally more responsive to the professionals who pass the time of day with them every week and donate generously to Christmas boxes. In the smaller rooms the porters also telephone particular dealers to report on upcoming sales, warning them of something particularly interesting or saving them a wasted journey if there is nothing worth viewing. The porters earn their reward in cash commission on executing bids for their dealer friends (because of the possibilities of bribery, porters have now been banned from accepting commission bids in most of the West End auctions). After the sale, a friendly porter can be extremely useful in keeping purchases back which might otherwise have been sent off to the auctioneer's warehouse, incurring a penalty charge on collection. Packing materials for breakables are also supplied free of charge to favoured traders.

At the larger rooms, the leading dealers enjoy the champagne benefits of invitations to private preview parties and to prestigious evening sales where useful contacts are made and a great deal of business concluded outside the auction itself. For the select few there are also those delightful boardroom luncheons where civilized conversation ranges across any subject rather than 'antiques'.

Dealers are also treated well as sellers at auction. When consigning goods for sale, they are given an automatic reduction on the vendor's commission, making them, at some auction houses, 30 per cent better off than private individuals. Knowing the ways of auctioneers, and the values of works of art, dealers are in a powerful position to negotiate further on the commission and on the extra charges which creep in under the line, such as photographic, insurance and advertising fees. No self-respecting dealer would tolerate billing for these fees, or for the buying-in commission should a work of art he owns fail to sell against a reserve recommended by the auctioneer. Quite a few influential dealers in London first cut their art market teeth by working for an auction house and the inside information they thus acquire enables them to strike a hard bargain when consigning important properties for sale on behalf of clients. They know all about 'net reserves' and about the extra business brought to the auction house as a result of publicity-catching sales, so threats to take a fine collection to the opposition are keenly felt. Such bargainers will also insist on their own considerable reward in terms of introductory commission, sometimes payable whether the property reaches its reserve or not. It must be maddening for the finance director of a leading auction house to pay out tens of thousands of pounds in introductory commission to an ex-employee for bringing back an important piece of business to the rooms which he had taken away with him when he left a few months earlier. The antiques trade is such a personal business that a collector's loyalty almost always remains with the individual, not with the institution for which he works; hence the pin-sticking and back-stabbing which occurs whenever a bright colleague leaves an Emporium or auction house to set up on his own.

Many of the best auctioneers are themselves dealers *manqué* and possess an admirable flair for promoting their sales in the press. One of the recent developments is for thematic auctions, and dealers are constantly pestered by auctioneers for consignments to fill the sails of becalmed catalogues. In persuading dealers to enter their stock in particular auctions, departmental heads are well aware of the obligations to make a profit for their commercial friends and complex arrangements are made to ensure decent prices. One of the main challenges is to conceal from other dealers the fact that a sale billed as 'Important' on the hard cover of a catalogue costing perhaps £10 actually contains too many trade properties weighted down by aggressive reserves fixed way above the encouraging estimates. Dealers loathe buying a work of art which they were unaware had been sitting in a rival's shop where it had been turned down by most of the likely collectors. Not all dealers' properties are 'old dogs', for they sometimes consign major discoveries straight to the rooms in the knowledge that a Japanese microchip magnate might turn up to compete against an Emirates petrochemical multimillionaire at many times the price he would dare ask in his shop. All the same, no really good dealer succumbs to this kind of temptation, always preferring to sell his best things privately to a fine collector of his own choice.

Some critics are suspicious of everything connected with the art market and believe that if the auctioneers are not buying lots cheaply for themselves at the expense of their clients, then they are somehow working in cahoots with their mates in the trade to defraud the public. In fact, as the auctioneer's only income is in commission on the hammer price, his interests are clearly identifiable with those of the vendor, namely to push prices as high as possible, whereas the dealer is normally trying to buy stock as cheaply as possible. In a sense, therefore, the dealer earns his living by buying bargains at the expense of the auctioneer, and the two actually spend much of the time in direct competition with each other.

The area where a good specialist dealer has the greatest opportunity of embarrassing the auction houses is in discovering wrongly catalogued masterpieces tucked away in minor sales unnoticed by anyone but himself. Dealers daydream about making the auction 'coup' which will settle their debts and establish their business on a secure financial footing for life. In November 1978 the dream became reality for one young dealer. On his weekly visit to a secondary saleroom the dealer was thumbing through a folder of miscellaneous prints and drawings when a small watercolour attracted his attention. Living near Petworth in Sussex, he had a passion for the watercolour sketches executed by Turner in the landscaped Park while staying with Lord Egremont: one of these impressionistic landscapes on blue paper seemed to have materialized before his eyes. The dealer took a hurried look at the masterful scrap of paper and shoved it back among the dross before any rival at his elbow could spot the cause of his excitement. It seemed too good to be true, and he hurried off to the British Museum to look through the main body of Petworth sketches which were presented to the nation by John Ruskin. Everything corresponded so precisely, so perfectly, in size and type of paper and in general style, that a fair assumption might have been that the saleroom discovery was a complete fake or, at best, a copy by one of Ruskin's students. Thinking about it overnight, however, the young dealer refused to relinquish his dream and he went along to the sale armed with his bank manager's indulgent permission to run up an overdraft of £10,000 if necessary. He did not need to – the watercolour was knocked down to him for only £50, despite the presence in the saleroom of many leading West End dealers. So far so good – too good in fact, because the young dealer now encountered great difficulty in securing any kind of coherent view from the scholars and museum experts whose opinion alone could turn his £50 'Turner' into a 'Joseph Mallord William Turner' worth thousands. After months of indecision, the chief Turner guru came out firmly in favour of its being a rare absconder from Ruskin's Petworth hoard, and with this scholarly support for his own belief in the watercolour the dealer set his business on the road to Bond Street by selling the Turner to the United States for over £30,000.

It is unusual for an uncatalogued rarity to pass through the London rooms without its being noticed by several dealers, leading to a hammer price bearing no relation to the modest estimate. Lots with an estimate of £30 or £40 which sell for thousands are called 'sleepers' by the auctioneer. Even when several members of the trade do cross swords over an innocent, unillustrated lot, the profits can still be good, as happened recently to another dealer who was forced to pay over £3,000 for a table estimated by a leading auction house at about £100. The dealer knew, as did his rival bidders, that the table was an unusual design by the architect C.F.A. Voysey; indeed it carried his cabinetmaker's label. In order to justify paying such a competitive price it would be necessary to supply documentary proof of the table's origins and the dealer needed to find out some information from the vendor. Nowadays the auctioneers refuse to tell the seller's name to the buyer for fear that further business will be done directly rather than through the rooms, and the most they will do is pass on a 'Dear Sir' letter. In this case a reply came back promptly from the owner saying that nothing was known about the history of the table except that it came from a house in Beaconsfield. This was all that was needed, as an original Voysey drawing of the table in the collection of the Royal Institute of British Architects indicated that two of these were made for Mr Burke's house 'Hollymount' in Beaconsfield. It was subsequently sold to a national museum at a substantial profit.

A good deal of luck as well as expertise is involved in making an auction room 'coup' in London where hundreds of dealers and collectors view each sale, and receive the

catalogues. The other day a chest of drawers painted by the important Victorian architect William Burges for his own house, a Gothic folly in Kensington, surfaced in a secondary saleroom in London. The week before, a wardrobe from the same house, correctly catalogued as coming from the collection of Evelyn Waugh, was sold by a major auction house for £45,000. Notwithstanding the publicity that had surrounded this price, a lucky dealer managed to purchase the chest of drawers for only £950 because a rival who was holding a commission bid for £8,000 failed to hear the lot being called and missed his bid! In the same week a clever dealer sold a Hoffmann silver spoon through the London rooms for over £16,000 – he had bought it nine months previously at another auction house a few hundred yards up the road in a job lot for £180. Amusingly, the dealer had been unable to find any takers in the trade at an asking price of £4,000, and the decision to put it into auction had been made as a last resort to raise some money! Ten years ago an inexperienced dealer discovered on the Portobello Road for £55 a bronze figure of 'Piety' by Sir Alfred Gilbert, the sculptor of the Eros fountain at Piccadilly Circus. It was very beautiful and he was sad to part with it, even though the £1,000 he sold it for went towards the purchase of another bargain, an untouched Victorian villa in Holland Park. In 1983 'Truth', the matching bronze to 'Piety', was offered at auction in London and fetched £10,000.

In every field of collecting such stories abound; they are all true in their essentials and the opportunities for making a 'coup' in the rooms will always be available to the experienced specialist with an eye and a mind of his own.

The private war between dealers and auctioneers is fought across many fronts. Some of the fiercest fighting at present is in the struggle to capture the soul of the collector.

Until well into the 1960s the general public was still in the pocket of the dealer, who upheld his position as an essential intermediary between collector and auctioneer despite having lost ground in other aspects of the trade. Flattering publicity given to auctions by newspapers and television in the early '70s encouraged some auctioneers to mount a relatively aggressive campaign to persuade the public to come direct to them both as buyers and as sellers. The appearance of more and more members of the public competing in the rooms is disturbing to dealers, as collectors are often willing to bid up to the full retail value, thus cutting the dealer out altogether as the middleman. Faced with the threat of being drummed out of business, many dealers have compromised by becoming little more than commission agents for clients at auction, earning their 5 per cent or whatever by detailed condition reports and advice on value. Other dealers fight the collectors by buying at virtually any cost the best works of art in their field at auction, thus eventually forcing the collector to back down if he wishes to buy again in the trade at an affordable price. Periodic fluctuations in the market are often due to this kind of bidding warfare rather than to any genuine revaluation of the field. Some dealers, though not on their strongest ground when it comes to discussing ethics, point out that the auctioneers are not morally justified in claiming to provide independent guidance to buyers when they act primarily for the sellers whose interests are identical with their own – namely to secure maximum prices. Judging auctioneers (perhaps wrongly though perhaps not) by their own standards, dealers suggest how much easier it must be to fix the reserves when one is also fixing the bids.

Dealers also maintain that the auctioneers adopt unprincipled tactics in securing consignments for sale by quoting very high prices and then reducing the estimates dramatically just before the sale when the private vendor is already too heavily committed to withdraw. The bold auctioneer, protected by the pages of small type on his conditions of sale, would probably also threaten to charge a withdrawal fee before giving the owner back his goods. Good dealers argue that collectors would be better advised to accept a reasonable offer from the trade rather than to wait six months for an appropriate auction and find that an optimistic estimate of £1,000 or so actually results in a hammer price of £600 and net sale proceeds after reduction of commission and expenses of less than £500. The story does not end there, argue the dealers, for the auctioneers insist on being paid by the buyer within three days, but refuse to pay the vendor for a calendar month, adding interest to their income. Trade organizations seek to explain to the public that the buyer's premium (10 per cent plus Value Added Tax on the hammer price at most London auctions) is in effect a further commission penalizing the vendor as dealers reduce their bids to allow for the fact that a hammer price of £600 actually costs them £669. It is fair to say that in many cases a good dealer would prefer to pay a collector £700 for a direct purchase rather than bid £600 at auction, making a net difference to the vendor of over £200. The reason for a dealer's willingness to pay privately slightly more than he would at auction is that it is easier to find buyers for a work of art that is fresh on the market.

As London dealers are still the dominant buyers in the rooms, their most potent method of legally controlling the auction outcome is to put together a consortium of bidders. This may sound like the dreaded 'ring' by another name, but a ruling in the High Court in 1982 pronounced that consortium bidding is legal, provided the auctioneer is informed before the sale of the names of the dealers who are acting together. The consortium is not obliged to disclose its hand any further by identifying which lots it might be after, nor by committing the participants to act in partnership throughout the sale. By definition an illegal ring occurs when a number of dealers come to a secret arrangement in the rooms not to bid against each other in order to depress the prices and to share the profits afterwards. Dealers have always argued that, whatever the strict legalities of the matter, auctions are fair game for any such arrangements because the auctioneer is paid by the vendor to be his agent and it is therefore his duty to protect the price by describing the object correctly, by advising a decent reserve, and by securing competitive bids from abroad. It could also be pointed out that a legal consortium may in fact have the illegal effect of depressing the price if the three or four leading international dealers in a particular field join forces when they would otherwise have been competing. The opposite is also true, that an illegal ring can lead to increased prices provided there is adequate competition from another quarter for, by pooling their resources, the 'boys' can bid higher than they would have been able to do as individuals.

The antiques market has grown so broad that the days are gone when the notorious London dealers' rings could really control prices in the rooms up and down the country. In fact the fire-power of the ring was defused some time ago by a remarkable *Sunday Times* article in November 1964, entitled 'The Curious Case of the Chippendale Commode'. This recorded the infiltration by reporters on two separate occasions of private auctions held after major public sales in order to 'knock out' the acquisitions of the ring. In each case the illegal auction was conducted by a committee member of the British Antique Dealers' Association, the Oxbridge of the tráde organizations, and was attended by many rank-and-file members among the fifty or so dealers present, all of whom had presumably sat on their hands during the public auction while items were sold to the ring's nominee bidder for a fraction of their full value. This marvellous piece of investigatory journalism inspired a debate in the House of Commons where the Member for Cirencester offered a typical parliamentarian's solution: 'The only way to kill these mosquitoes is to drain the swamp in which they breathe.' 'Here! Here!', was no doubt the reply.

The standard practice these days, indulged in by many members of the trade though strictly illegal, is part-share buying. Through enquiries over the telephone or upon meeting in the rooms, two, three and more dealers discover that they are all after the same piece of furniture. The lot may be correctly catalogued but with a tiny estimate indicating a low reserve, or it may be wrongly catalogued altogether; either way, the dealers reckon it could come away very cheaply if they do not bid against each other. So they form an unofficial consortium, one of them buying the lot and invoicing his colleagues for their share in the purchase price and subsequent selling costs such as restoration, transportation, and research. The piece of furniture is then passed from dealer to dealer until it sells, the proceeds being split in the same proportions. This kind of arrangement can only work among dealers who know each other and trust that the one handling the sale will be honest about the price secured. Also, it is worth doing only if the potential profit is very large and the dealers would each have had the money and knowledge to bid aggressively on their own account; otherwise, the dominant dealer is better off buying the piece against his colleagues and keeping all the profit himself. Some dealers take the view that part-share buying is not worth while with more than one other person – that is, on a half-share basis – and even then they would much rather not be drawn into any such arrangements. There is something unsavoury, distinctly distasteful, about respectable dealers owning third and fourth shares in numerous items of stock scattered about the London trade.

And part-share buying frequently deteriorates into some form of knock out, no activity for any self-respecting dealer. The simplest type of knock out is between two dealers, with everything agreed before the marked lot comes to the rostrum. A sixteenth-century pewter flagon in a country sale may be catalogued as nineteenth-century and two London dealers, having breakfasted very early in order to get to the sale on time, curse their luck in finding the other one there as well. Over a cup of coffee, manoeuvres are made by each of them to discover what the other one thinks the flagon is worth, and the more bullish dealer may end up announcing that his maximum price is £600 and that he will pay his colleague half the difference between this and the hammer price if he does not bid. The chances are that his maximum bid will be much more than this, but if the other dealer has neither the guts nor the money to call his bluff, the arrangements stands. A provincial dealer or two are bound to have spotted the flagon, and despite an estimate of £50–£80 it may well cost £400 and the buyer pays off his colleague with £100 in cash. When the two dealers involved have equal respect for each other's knowledge the more likely scenario is for one of them to buy the flagon on the understanding that the other retains an option to buy it after the sale, or to be bought out. The second dealer may say that his buying or selling-out price is £800, and if the first dealer wants to keep the flagon he has to pay his friend another £400 on top of the auction price. The flagon therefore costs no less than if they had bid against each other at the auction, but friendly specialists prefer to give each other a profit rather than the auctioneer. There is also the point that by not bidding publicly against each other neither the auctioneer nor the provincial dealers learn what the London experts consider the flagon to be worth. The richer dealer secures a rarity for which he may have an immediate client at £1,500, and the poorer dealer himself becomes richer to the sum of £400 without having laid out a penny.

As the knock out is seldom quite so simple as this, one wonders why the more powerful, wealthier dealers bother to operate the system. The reasons are similar to those for insider-dealing: lack of liquidity and fraternal self-protection. Even dealers with large credit facilities through banks or private backers have some kind of limit to their liquidity and would eventually have to stop buying if they were always forced to pay the top prices. Dealers who have the knowledge but not the money find themselves permanent underbidders, taking away from the profits of other dealers, boosting the coffers of the auction houses, and not making any money for themselves. Many dealers – most dealers, it is fair to say – decide that they would prefer to be paid off in some form for not bidding publicly and thus earn a certain amount of money rather than go on under-bidding and earn nothing at all. The bigger dealers become involved in the knock out in order to save money and not to fall out with some of the smaller dealers who are important suppliers to them of goods bought in the country. And there is simply the traditional loyalty of the trade, the established code discussed earlier whereby dealers instinctively stick together in the belief that they all rely on each other's prosperity at whatever level of the trade. The barons of the trade, the kings of the ring, also like to have other dealers tied to their purse strings and compromised by participation in the knock out, for that reduces the risks of damaging disclosures to the press.

In certain areas of the art market, rings of London dealers still operate on a relatively large scale, though killings are less frequent and there is often little extra profit left to divide up on the important lots which are competed for heavily by rival 'consortiums', foreign dealers, and the growing number of private collectors attending auctions. It is difficult to find out exactly how the rings function these days, as the private post-sale auction has been replaced by more secretive methods of sorting out the spoils. It seems that minor members of a ring are first paid off with a small cash bribe, leaving perhaps between three and six contenders for the ringed purchases. The occasional sight of a car parked in a side street near a provincial saleroom stuffed with London dealers shuffling pieces of paper and punching pocket calculators leads one to suspect that some kind of sealed bidding system operates. Anyway, whatever the method of reaching a conclusion, the dealer who ends up with each piece has to pay off his colleagues in proportion to the prices which they claim to have been prepared to pay at the auction. It is apparently a nerve-racking business as dealers in the knock out steel themselves to make the highest offers they dare in order to maximize their earnings without actually buying anything; stories are told of over-clever dealers being virtually bankrupted by other members of the ring who gang up to land them with the goods at excessive prices.

On occasion the police have successfully prosecuted provincial auctioneers for participating in the knock out after sales in their own auction rooms, and though such things could not happen in any major auction house many auctioneers in effect condone the activities of the ring by default. The members of established rings are perfectly well known to the auctioneer and the operation of a ring is normally signalled clearly by huddled groups before the sale and by a certain amount of gesticulating, even shouting, during the sale, and yet only on one occasion has a London auctioneer brought a case to court against the ring. Some auctioneers argue that it would be too difficult to provide witnesses and evidence sufficient to prosecute a case of ringing, but this is simply not true, as tape-recordings are taken of every sale in the major rooms and security cameras film much of what is going on; and there is the additional circumstantial evidence of lots being switched from one dealer's bill to another after the sale, as well as the appearance of the ring-leader's auction purchases in his neighbour's shop when that neighbour had attended the sale but not bid. The auctioneers turn a blind eye to the activities of the ring because they wish to avoid any kind of public scandal in the art market which might threaten confidence and stability. Vendors would be reluctant to consign goods for sale if auctioneers admitted that dealers' rings operated successfully to deflate prices, and private buyers would be frightened away from the salerooms by the image which would be given in newspaper reports of marauding gangs of criminal dealers. Perhaps auctioneers take the stoical view that it is their job to protect clients by providing correct reserves, not by resorting to the courts-of-law.

There is a considerable amount of legitimate gamesmanship in the way professionals conduct themselves in the saleroom, especially when an independent specialist plots to conceal his full intentions both from the auctioneer and from rival bidders so that others may not benefit from his expertise. There are marked dealers in every field whose reputations are such that if they are seen to be bidding on something, others assume it must be a work of distinction and therefore have a go themselves. One of the older London furniture dealers is so well known in the trade for buying good things at reasonable prices that several young men have set their businesses going on the right road by watching the old man in the rooms and never bidding on pieces for which he declined to make an offer. Provided the old boy does not run his young competitors up to teach them a lesson, anything bought for one bid more than his is still a good buy. The simplest way to avoid this kind of competition from the floor of the room is to leave commission bids with the auctioneer, but he too will be influenced by the specialist's interest in a particular lot and may be inspired to do some last-minute research before the auction, which will be made known to other dealers and collectors. Subtler means of protection must be found.

The clearest way of illustrating how it works is to take an example. The auctioneer fails to ascribe the architect's name to an interesting model of a country house, accurate information on which would make it worth five times the modest estimate of £400–500. Before the sale there is a certain amount of speculation in the trade as to the authorship of the model, but no definite attribution emerges; and on the day of the sale educated attention is focused on the two or three specialists who have the expertise to make a valid judgment. As everyone will be expecting the architectural specialist at least to do something about the model if only for speculation, one way of putting other dealers off the scent is for him to bid ostentatiously up to £450, then to drop out of the bidding with dismissive shakes of the head and pretend to take no further interest in the proceedings. In fact, the specialist's cousin or daughter-in-law, someone whose face is not known to the trade, has been instructed to continue bidding up to £1,800 on his behalf. If the bidding goes beyond that figure there is no hiding the fact that it is a model of some significance and above £1,800 the specialist perfers to bid for himself, partly because of his experienced bidding technique, and partly because he may still not have decided exactly how much he is prepared to pay, for the final judgment of value, even in his case, also depends on who else wants it. A cool, calculating bidder delays entering the fray until the hammer is about to fall, and the bids are offered slowly and self-confidently with many a steely look around the room at other bidders. The auctioneer will try to keep the pace going and stop the specialist from staring his competitors into submission.

Alternatively, some specialists prefer to stand in a dark corner at the back of the room waiting for the right moment to attract the auctioneer's attention with a flick of the catalogue, and thereafter register the bids with a minute raising of the eyebrow. Dealers near the front who turn round to see who is bidding cannot hope to follow the direction of the auctioneer's glance to a discreet eyebrow hiding in the crowd; in this case the specialist will want the bidding to mount quickly so that others lose heart and fall out of the race, afraid that no one else is really bidding at all and that the auctioneer is running them up against the reserve.

The specialist or eminent collector might finally be reduced to engaging the auctioneer's connivance in hoodwinking the opposition with a secret bidding code. One California collector has made such a name for himself over the years as a code bidder that it can now be assumed on his

rare personal appearances in the saleroom that he is bound to be bidding on the major lot whenever it seems that he is not. In 1965 such confusion arose during a major London auction that the collector was forced to read out a letter of agreement between himself and the auctioneer which went as follows: 'When Mr "X" is sitting down he is bidding. If he bids openly he is bidding. When he stands up he has stopped bidding. If he sits down again he is not bidding until he raises his finger. Having raised his finger he is bidding until he stands up again.' This arrangement was so fiendishly complicated that the auctioneer, in the heat of the moment, was unable to follow the instructions and mistakenly knocked the lot down to someone else. Dealers go for simpler codes, and a specialist may tell the auctioneer that when a particular lot comes up he will be standing in the very centre of the room behind the last row of chairs and whenever he scratches the back of his head he should be considered to be bidding. It would thus be possible for the specialist to stand with his back to the rostrum, engage his chief rival in heated conversation, and at the same time buy a coveted, under-catalogued rarity by scratching the back of his head. The trick will be completed by the auctioneer calling out an agreed pseudonym rather than the dealer's name. The use of a pseudonym is particularly important when the dealer is bidding secretly against one of his own clients, either on his own account or on behalf of a rival collector. One of the problems for a specialist is that several clients may wish him to bid for the same lot in order to remove him from the competition and also to solicit his advice on value; all explanations can be avoided by refusing commission bids and bidding secretly.

Those are some of the legitimate tricks of the saleroom, all of which receive tacit approval from the auctioneer, and some of which require his actual support. Other things go on in the rooms which the auctioneer makes every effort to eliminate. At the viewing, unscrupulous dealers have been known to lock the fall-front of a particularly attractive secretaire à abattant and pocket the key. Unless one of the porters happens to be an amateur locksmith, the secretaire is likely to be sold relatively cheaply to the man who has stolen the key. While the porters' backs are turned the same kind of dealer may try to hide one of a pair of embroidered curtains he is interested in, or to push out of sight a rare medallion in an otherwise undistinguished lot. And there is the non-criminal but no less despicable technique of spreading false rumours that the major lot in a sale is a fake, then sending an unknown nominee to buy a masterpiece cheaply. Bad-mouthing of this sort can be effective only from the tongue of an acknowledged expert, whose alternative method of putting people off bidding is to tell the world that there is a vast bid from the National Trust and it would therefore not only be pointless for rivals to bid but would be considered discourteous to force such a worthy institution to pay more than the minimum. What, one is entitled to ask, about the poor owner when this happens? And what about rival dealers when Mr. Hearsay persuades them not to bid and the object turns up after the sale in the slick-speaking specialist's shop? 'Oh, the National Trust. Were they meant to be bidding? I never heard that rumour.'

Devious dealers can also catch the auctioneers out when they are selling through the rooms as well as in buying. It is well known that dealers pass their dubious purchases and clever restorations through certain so-called experts in the London auction rooms who know no better than to catalogue these geese as swans. The ineptitude of particular auctioneers is compounded by the dishonesty of some members of the trade who encourage trusting clients to bid on works of art they own themselves and know to be false. Some dealers also use the rooms as a means of selling their decent stock to those customers who are prepared to pay more at a public auction than in an antique shop. It is a way of catching out these suspicious clients who are naive enough to imagine that open competition in the rooms guarantees real value, however high the price. The dealer delivers his goods to the saleroom on the understanding that he will agree to whatever reserve is suggested provided a high estimate is published; when the catalogue is printed the dealer points out the relevant lot to his client as something which might be of interest, persuades him to leave an enormous commission bid, and then rings up the auctioneer at the last moment before the sale to raise his reserve accordingly. The client does not know that the lot belongs to the dealer, and the auctioneer does not realize that the dealer knows the commission bidder. Knowing that the lot is going to sell on commission, the auctioneer would have to be a shining white knight to refuse to raise the reserve for an influential dealer under these circumstances. Although it is against the law for an owner to bid on his own lot below the reserve, this does not deter some dealers from organizing a placeman to bid until just below an excessive reserve, thus establishing a high price without necessarily achieving a sale. Settlement of the buying-in charge is little to pay for creating a new price structure in a field where the dealer is well stocked. This is called 'puffing', a practice which is rightly and roundly condemned by the auctioneers whenever they suspect it might be happening. Auctioneers also keep a careful watch on any dealers who might send a placeman to the auction to buy their lots at high prices under a false name and address, in the hope that the auctioneers will be foolish enough to pay out the vendor's proceeds without having collected from the false buyer.

The gentlemanly elegance of the major London auction rooms belies the cut-throat nature of the business, and an honest dealer must keep his wits sharp as he goes about his daily business in the rooms. There is a lot to see, and London furniture dealers have between ten and fifteen auctions to view every week in town before venturing out to the often excellent provincial sales. A well-organized dealer manages to avoid unnecessary tussles with the London traffic by packing his viewing into two separate sessions of intense activity. Each dealer has his own unchanging route, starting at the rooms nearest to his home and incorporating calls at various shops on the way. The narrow specialist seldom bothers to buy a catalogue for the minor sales, being interested only in the odd esoteric object; weeks can pass without his seeing a single piece which attracts more than passing attention and the single-minded specialist can view a five-hundred lot sale in a couple of minutes without breaking step. But it is not simply a question of looking at the sale; there are deals to be discussed with other morning viewers, porters and auctioneers to pass the time of day with, the previous week's purchases perhaps to be collected, and endless necessary rituals to be observed.

The first thing a dealer needs to learn about the business of viewing the London auction rooms is where best to leave his car without incurring a parking fine. Side streets and backyards near the London auction rooms witness the continuous coming and going each week of the same mud-spattered cars with their back seats folded down to accommodate the tell-tale tools of the dealer's trade: cardboard boxes, crumpled newspaper, and protective eiderdowns. At the larger salerooms dealers emerge from all corners of the

compass, through side-doors, from goods lifts, up the main stairs, down the back stairs, into the viewing gallery where the furniture is set out in spacious order. There is plenty of room to turn tables on their end and look for cabinetmaker's marks, or to pile the drawers of tallboys on the floor and inspect the carcase for restoration. If a stretcher or piece of beading is missing, the dealer will quiz one of the porters to see if there is any chance of its turning up, thus avoiding the time and expense of taking it to a restorer. On a particularly puzzling piece a dealer may wish to discuss ideas with the cataloguer or with a colleague who happens to pass. The accumulation of years of dirt and bleaching from the sun can make it difficult to identify the wood, and as date and country of origin are sometimes by no means certain either, two opinions are always better than one. Dealers at the view

can be seen making quick sketches of coats of arms, collectors' ciphers, unfamiliar trade labels and other identifying marks which can be researched before the sale, perhaps leading to an attribution. Lot numbers are noted with price assessments in code at the side; names of potential customers are scribbled in the margins to remind the dealer to make an exploratory telephone call before the sale; damage is noted, the cost of restoration assessed, and carriers are alerted.

At smaller auction rooms, antique furniture is piled up to the ceiling along with the 'household effects' and viewing is more hazardous. Grey-suited West End specialists clamber across suites of bedroom furniture to open the drawers of bonheur de jours at the top of the stack – like plain-clothed detectives searching for stolen state secrets in Ealing Studios movies. Trouble looms around every corner. Where is the lost chair from a set of six, was the top of the table scratched before or after the hammer fell, can the porter be trusted with a high commission bid, is there some plot to sabotage the phone booths, has any rival in disguise spotted the hidden rarity, will the hero be crushed beneath an avalanche of toppling tea-tables?

The larger general furniture dealers as well as the shippers spend much longer viewing each sale than do the narrow specialists. There is a wide range of goods that they are prepared to buy if the price is right, and they have to mark their maximum bids on over half the lots in the sale even though they may end up bidding on no more than a dozen and buying only five. Sometimes there is so much to do in the shop that the dealer is forced to view after the auction has already started, and he pushes his way through the milling crowds to look at an interesting table at the other side of the room while the hammer hovers at no money at all. Is it perhaps riddled with woodworm, he wonders, and are the legs original? Too late, the hammer falls and a rival's name is called out as the buyer. Every auction contains several lots which sell cheaply on the day, and this is where the good dealer reaps his rewards for careful viewing every week of all the London sales.

Attitudes to buying at auction vary from dealer to dealer. At one extreme are the dealers who sit all the way through auction after auction and only bid on the bargains. At the other extreme are those who time their arrival at the auction for a few minutes before the one lot they have marked and bid aggressively on this and nothing else. The thinking behind the first approach is that if things are cheap enough they can always be sold at a profit, and behind the second that if they are good enough it does not matter about price.

Both attitudes can be mistaken because the secret of the trade is in the selling, not in the buying. In the middle of the road is the dealer who never buys anything at all at auction unless he can think of a specific client for it, either a fellow trader not attending the sale or a private collector. Such dealers have minds divided into pigeon-holes containing photographic images of the requirements of all their contacts and clients. Their skill lies in the understanding of other people's taste; they need have none of their own. The most successful dealers combine all these various qualities – they have the knowledge to bid strongly on the finest things; they have the breadth of business to buy amusing things which are going cheap; and as their passion in life is buying and selling they market as much as they can as fast as they can. It is dealers like these whose names are called out lot after lot in sale after sale in the London auction rooms until their competitors give up trying to work out how they possibly sell it all. Their businesses grow bigger and bigger and the vast value of their stock makes them paper-rich; but it is money that they never see for themselves because they continue dealing until death overtakes them, consumed by their passion for the market place.

These dedicated, single-minded dealers are the biggest buyers at auction, but the best buyers, in a sense the best dealers in every way, are the independent specialists who bid selectively on the strength of their private knowledge and personal taste. There is a certain amount of arrogance and conceit in the way these individualists ignore the opinions and estimates of the auctioneers and dismiss offers of part-share and consortium bidding from other dealers. The solid conservative centre of the trade finds them dangerously unconventional in their attitudes to the shibboleths of the business and fears their outspoken disrespect for the code of secrecy. Theirs are the premises which are like no one else's, theirs the stock with peculiar qualities, theirs the clients who are also friends. They too are the buyers best equipped to circumnavigate the many pitfalls that disfigure the market place as a result of the intricate relationship which exists between dealer and auctioneer.

Five

Motives and Issues

'It has become the mode to have taste, private galleries in New York are becoming almost as common as private stables.' So said a wealthy American picture collector, James Jackson Jarvis, towards the end of the last century. A hundred years before, in the 1780s, participation in art market activities was equally a mark of breeding, and the young lady of fashion found that 'in one continual hurry rolled her days,/at routs, assemblies, auctions, op'ras, plays/ . . . she rises with the sun and Christie's sees her aking head at one.' Two centuries since the time when Charles Jenner was thus conducting aspiring socialites through the rigours of London life, antiques have become yet more fashionable and smart daughters of jet-set parents queue up for courses 'at the V and A, darling'.

Society and all its fashions have in modern times become far more accessible to the less well-off as well as to the less well-born. Industrial sophistication, speed of communication and increased social mobility make it impossible for any fashion to remain exclusive for more than a week or two. No sooner are the latest designs of the newest Japanese whizz-kid draped across the shoulders of wealthy trend-setters, than High Street shops produce acceptable imitations for the eager followers of fashion. It is the same with today's fad for antiques. Connoisseurship is no longer the idle prerogative of much-travelled aesthetes, and collecting antiques is open to all. In the eighteenth century, antiquarian interest was confined to a small section of the educated aristocracy. In the nineteenth century, collecting works of art came to be dominated by the nouveaux riches, first through fortunes made in the Old World by the Rothschilds, the Holloways and their like, and later by the New World wealth of the Vanderbilts, the Rockefellers and other American collectors. In the twentieth century, more social barriers have been torn or taken down, and collecting has become a popular sport, played by large numbers of people and watched by many more. Even at a market stall, everyone can participate in the popular fashion for collecting. Whether spending a lot of money or little, more than half the people in London who buy antiques do so because it is a popular way of using leisure time and because revivalist styles in interior decoration are the recommended fashion.

All this has happened relatively quickly. No so long ago it would have been considered wildly eccentric for a stockbroker in Guildford to eat off unmatching majolica plates instead of a modern Royal Doulton dinner service, or for a teenager in Hounslow to spend his savings on a phonograph and cylinder records rather than a sophisticated hi-fidelity system. Nowadays the nostalgia boom reaches right down to the teeny-boppers, many of whom dress up in second-hand clothes and collect the pop memorabilia of their parents' youth. Rebellious art students turn their backs on abstract and minimalist trends in the modern movement and return to the traditional ideas of William Morris and the Arts and Crafts revival. General respect for the art and artefacts of the past is reflected in the work of many leading architects and designers whose use of earlier forms and ideas often displays pedantic antiquarian accuracy. Brick buildings hark back to the Victorian vernacular of Philip Webb, type-faces reach for the academic excellence of Eric Gill, and printed fabrics plagiarize the colours and shapes of the Art Deco period. Old-fashioned and ultra-modern have become almost the same thing – antiques are barely old, and contemporary fashion is barely new.

Interest in antiques is located throughout all sections of the community. Taxi-drivers and cabinet ministers keep weekly appointments with their television sets to watch 'The Antiques Roadshow', which is often among the top ten in the ratings alongside 'Coronation Street' and the 'Nine O'Clock News'. The stately homes draw larger and larger crowds of admiring visitors every year, and books on antiques, on restoring, and on period decoration are bought in huge numbers. Now that some of the mystique and the exclusiveness of the art and antiques market has been removed, people are less frightened about taking part; and at the same time the extension of collecting subjects virtually to the present day makes the whole scene more accessible and easier to relate to. It is worth looking for explanations for this rather surprising phenomenon of almost all sections of Western society turning away from experimental contemporary styles.

It has been suggested that the destructiveness of two world wars in Europe this century has made people respect what remains from the past simply because it survived against such odds. Eagerness to preserve the past may also be seen as a feeble gesture of human protest against the unfaceable horrors of nuclear destruction. Some psychologists argue that a natural fear is growing within society that scientific and industrial progress may actually be doing more harm than good, and instead of buying furniture and decorations in modern synthetic materials many people are, in effect, surrounding themselves with the products of earlier generations as a form of self-protection. The popularity of antiques certainly does not seem to be a pure statement of aesthetic preference for the styles of the past, for very few people possess a clear enough visual understanding to make such definite judgments. Intellectual and psychological stimulus is undoubtedly more important than visual satisfaction to most people, even in the collecting of antiques. One reason why the fashion for collecting has caught on may be that it satisfies a natural historical curiosity; certainly genuine interest in the function of an object and in how it was made can be gathered from the kind of questions asked by Saturday crowds at market stalls.

But whatever the underlying psychological motivations might be, there can be no doubt of the fact that the acquisition of 'antiques' is considered by most sections of the community to be an admirable activity. The houses of the fashionable rich who employ London decorators and the homes of suburban housewives who read the Sunday colour supplements display a similar popular interest in antiques, both as furnishing and as a basis for the style of interior decoration. The antique look is as much in fashion as antiques themselves. In modern kitchens, cupboard doors in formica are being replaced by heavily moulded pine doors with traditional brass handles. Gas fires in the smoke-free zones of the inner cities are now constructed to simulate log fires in mock-Georgian grates, a style which was ridiculed by popular taste a few years ago. Yesterday's failures, such as pottery flying ducks or wire furniture, have become today's treasured antiques. It could be argued that embracing the past in this uncritical way is a reflection of the innate conservative taste of British society, and it may well be true that the mass fashion for all things old is one of the many factors contributing to the dull, reactionary nature of public attitudes in Great Britain to the contemporary arts.

This kind of buying, guided by fashion and manipulated by the magazines, should not be called collecting. They may claim to be collectors, but these buyers make their purchases without any clear personal direction and with knowledge of nothing but popular taste. Bits and pieces of different styles, dates and countries of origin are acquired in order to create the approved decorative ambience, not for any intrinsic quality of their own. The last thing which matters about a particular earthenware vase destined for the drawing-room mantelpiece is who designed it – for some people price is of no concern and colour is the deciding factor; for others the colour is immaterial provided the price is low enough and the name of a well-known manufacturer can be quoted to friends. The market is dominated at all levels by people whose principal pleasure is derived from the impression their 'antiques' make on others.

At the top end of the market, works of art have become so expensive that genuine collectors are forced to dig into capital and therefore look upon their purchases as part of an overall investment portfolio. Before the Slump of the 1930s there were still quite a number of American and European industrialists whose income from wholly owned private companies and judicious investment was so large that they could afford to spend millions of dollars a year on luxurious collections without eating into capital. In the 1980s almost the only people in the world who can buy regularly at the top end of the market on their personal income are those connected with the international oil business. The rest of the money for buying masterpieces in different fields of the fine and decorative arts comes from some form of capital investment. Various different structures for art market investment have been devised. Some families in the United States whose wealth was founded on steel, railways and other heavy industries have formed private trusts owning existing collections and endowed with money for new purchases. Some of these trusts or 'foundations' run their own museums, which are open to the public and, unlike most state museums, quite frequently sell works of art from the collections. Other owners have hived off their possessions into investment companies registered in one of the international tax havens such as Panama, Liechtenstein, Jersey, the Cayman Islands, the Dutch Antilles or Monaco. Some collectors are so fearful of punitive taxation that they physically export all their works of art from their countries of residence, while others remain comfortably seated in Belgravia on their Chippendale chairs though they no longer officially own them. Anyone who buys regularly at the top end of the market is unlikely to be short of income and may indeed seldom need to realize capital on the works of art purchased; but in the final analysis such collectors are bound to look upon their activities in the salerooms and emporiums as a form of long-term capital investment, however passionate they may be about their subject. More and more collectors these days are motivated above all else by the idea of making a secure capital investment, and skill in the management of money now runs hand in hand with judgment about works of art.

There are many distressing features about the increasing dominance of the investor. During times of financial pressure on productive industries and shortage of investment in areas of direct social benefit, it is difficult to defend the expenditure of, for example, nearly £2 million on a suit of armour. It is even more difficult to answer socialist critics of the art market when prices are being pushed up to these heights by competing investors chasing works of art instead of more productive forms of investment. Fashionable works of art have never been cheap and in the welcome freedom of a political democracy people are able to spend their taxed income as they wish. There is, however, something to be said for structuring the art market in such a way that investors are penalized for spending such large sums of money on personal luxuries which no one has been paid to produce, which are valueless to the community at large, and which tie up capital in unproductive circumstances.

With any luck, the market itself will in due course punish the pure investor. The long-term stability of the market and its capacity to perform in financial terms depends on the passionate desire of individual collectors to possess a particular object for aesthetic, historical or any other reason than investment. Once more than a certain percentage of decisions in the international antiques market are made from investment criteria, prices will cease to have any solid basis and antiques will begin to fluctuate in value just like any other investment-controlled commodity where people buy in and out of the market for purely financial reasons. Investors will then find that the continuous inflation-beating performance over the last fifty years of French furniture suddenly breaks down, and the capacity of art-market gold mines like netsuke to quadruple their value in as many years fades away. If investors looked critically at the true investment performance of antiques they would discover that the market is less profitable than journalistic propaganda might suggest. The fact that certain pieces of Worcester porcelain or Kyoto shibayama record fantastic price increments in disposals at particular auctions does not mean that all examples can be sold as successfully. There are many problems. In the first place, auctions are a long time in preparation, success is not guaranteed, and high expenses and commissions are charged. No two objects are ever quite the same and the circumstances of disposal are always different, so there is no mechanism for accurate valuation in the antiques market. The graphs which analysts produce from time to time in order to convince wary investors that works of art are a field worth considering alongside property and land never allow for mistaken buys, those purchases which actually go down in value, either because they turn out to be forgeries or restorations, or because a dealer charged an exorbitant price for an accredited rarity which was later discovered to be relatively common. Analysts of stocks and shares chart the falls as well as the rises, but antiques market pundits tend to argue their case from the lowest purchase prices to the record sales prices. Promoters of art as investment fail to take proper account of the considerable expenses involved in servicing an investment portfolio in antiques – there is the cost of insurance, the losses through damage and theft, the costs of restoration and carriage, the employment of experts for authentication and agents to bid or negotiate, the payment of capital gains tax, the financial limitations of tying up capital in a non-income earning investment unacceptable as collateral for other business activities or overdrafts, and the dire lack of liquidity in disposal or transference of ownership, as well as the purely physical difficulties of movement.

This is not to deny that some very impressive art-market investments have been made, mostly by people buying with the knowledge and the eyes of a collector in undervalued fields. An American businessman living in Paris spotted the potential first of Art Nouveau and then of Art Deco before either field became popular; indeed he financed the whole of his initial Deco buying by selling a few pieces of Nouveau which he had bought for next to nothing in the early '60s. He took the view that the collecting establishment had failed to appreciate the quality and beauty of the period and so went out to buy the best at what dealers considered to be satisfactorily high prices at the time. The businessman, however, had researched the subject carefully enough to know what was rare as well as what was good, a distinction which dealers were unable to make and therefore unable to charge a differential for. Once Art Nouveau had become the international fashion and books had been published on the subject, it was discovered that the American businessman's collection contained nothing but documented and exhibited masterpieces worth enormous sums of money. Unsatisfied by this success and under cover of Nouveau madness, he proceeded to do exactly the same with Art Deco. The only way he could work the same trick again would be by adopting a total twenty-four hour disguise, for the eyes of the trade now follow his every move and a study is made of every purchase he makes in Paris, London and New York.

The other fact which commentators tend to ignore is that many of the people who realize gigantic profits in the art market paid a great deal of money for their purchases in the first place. Further proof is supplied of the adage 'money makes money'. When the Reverend Theodore Pitcairn sold his Monet 'La Terrasse à Saint-Adresse' in 1967 for £588,000, the press could have laid more emphasis on the fact that the original purchase price of $11,000 in 1926 could only have been afforded by a very rich man. Pitcairn was not simply the innocent pastor of the Lord's New Church of Bryn Athyn, he was also son of the founder of the Pittsburgh Glass Company, and his remarks at the time of the sale should be seen in this light: 'My wife and I were walking down 57th Street and saw it in a dealer's window. We bought it in ten minutes for about eleven thousand dollars. I wasn't thinking of investment. We were both struck by its cheerful quality and thought this was the type of picture that would always give us a lift'! It certainly did that, though the true profits are very much less than they might seem because of multiple reductions in purchasing power and by comparison with compound interest at bank rate of a forty-year investment.

Whether or not they are prepared to admit it, wealthy individuals today are bound to take account of the investment position in expenditure of their capital in the art market. Investors may become genuine and knowledgeable collectors but in the final analysis their possessions are always valued in financial terms as part of their capital wealth to be disposed of should the world economic climate so dictate. Pure collectors only sell works of art in order to finance other purchases or because they can no longer afford to insure them; any money they earn in this way is looked upon not for its investment potential but for the power it gives them to possess particular works of art.

Another motive for buying works of art, almost at the opposite end of the scale from investment, is house furnishing. Young couples setting up home on a low budget frequently decide that the prettiest and cheapest things can be found in small antique shops and minor auctions instead of modern stores. This practical initiation into the market place can be the foundation of a life-long interest in antiques. Judgments which are first made on functional grounds and on price considerations become more sophisticated and informed so that style, period and rarity begin to affect decisions and another addict becomes hooked on the drug of collecting. The framework for such collectors is their house and nothing can be bought which does not have a necessary function or specific decorative contribution within the home setting. This does not mean that everything need have period uniformity; far from it in fact, for many such collections are delightful for their individuality and stylistic contradictions. There is a tendency towards overcrowding and the academically inclined may litter their homes with historical allusions and weird juxtapositions, but the atmosphere remains personal and pleasurable. Intellectually pompous such a collector might perhaps be, but aesthetically over-refined he is definitely not, and nothing in his home would ever be isolated in spotlit splendour. As has been seen, fashion-conscious buyers also purchase antiques for the limited environment of their own home, but smart lighting and clever interior design features are used to attract the attention of visitors to the most expensive acquisitions. Genuine collectors express their own characters in furnishing a house, not cardboard ideals culled from fashion magazines lying about in dentists' waiting rooms.

The focal point of some collections is entirely historical, their aim being to illustrate a technical process, or to follow a particular theme through the periods, or to accumulate works of art and memorabilia surrounding one famous individual. The search and subsequent research are as important as the objects themselves, and these collectors spend more time looking at their card indexes and reference libraries than they do at their collections. They are the fanatics who accumulate enough information about their chosen subjects to fill dozens of ill-written manuals; indeed, in many cases they know more than anyone else in the world about topics which are too obscure and peripheral to attract the attention of museum curators and professional historians. Collectors of this kind are seldom extrovert characters. They are those shadowy figures who haunt the street markets and minor auctions rummaging through boxes of miscellanea and digging out anything they can find which can nourish their manias. The extent of such a collection, perhaps its very existence, may not be known to the trade until the collector dies and his life's work appears in an amazing auction catalogue – 350 lots of Wellingtonia amounting to 5,000 separate items of ephemera, commemorative ware, lithographs, books, bronzes, battle mementoes, personal memorabilia and anything else relating to the Iron Duke's long life; sixty lots illustrative of the history of hydraulic pump engines covering rare working models of the different systems, makers' plates, original drawings by engineers including perhaps the presentation folders for Tower Bridge, photographs, letters, patents, manuscripts and all the rest; a single catalogue devoted to Death and incorporating a mourning jewellery collection from Renaissance times to the Edwardian period, hangmen's tools and assassins' weapons, carved ivory skulls from Japan, cats' coffins from Cairo, endless ephemera including death certificates and funeral parlour advertisements, and masses of other ghoulish keepsakes.

Fanatical collectors in this category plan all their free time around the pursuit of Wellington, pump engines and Death. Evenings are spent researching, weekends searching, and holidays on pilgrimages to foreign parts – the first collector to the fields of Waterloo, the second to the engineeriums of Leningrad, and the third to the death camps of Dachau and Buchenwald. They have no concern for aesthetic quality, only for what is historically significant by their criteria; few of these collections have any visual appeal and many of them are considered to be somewhat limited and tasteless.

A surprising number of collectors with other motivations also fail to make aesthetic judgments despite the fact that 'antiques' (furniture, ceramics, textiles, silver, jewellery, watches, etc.) are contained within the broad heading of 'the decorative arts'. There is, to take another example, the type of collector who cares more than anything else about the rarity of an object within his chosen field and therefore makes no distinction between ugliness and beauty, so long as a newly acquired Staffordshire figure is previously unrecorded or an enamel snuff box has an unheard-of form of marking. It is not that they forgive a rarity for its aesthetic failings, they just do not see or think in those terms. Some of these collectors spend more time admiring the back of a plate for its marvellous marks than they do looking at the decoration on the front; they can be as pleased to own the rare original packaging as the object itself. Individuals who approach works of art in this technical way tend to pick on subjects which lend themselves to text-book collecting, such as stamps, pot-lids, coins, toys, and illustrated books, where detailed listings can be made and the rarities recorded. The aim in many of these fields is to acquire an example of every known shape or form and of all the variants in marks and decoration; the pride of this type of collection will be any piece which is accepted as being unique, regardless of its physical significance. Under these circumstances competition at auction between two established collectors for an unrecorded example leads to enormous prices. It is an amusing reversal of fortune for these objects – among the manufactured decorative arts such as porcelain and glass, it is the unsuccessful lines which are now rare and valuable but which at the time were made in small numbers because the design was judged by the buying public to be ugly or the manufacture seen to be inferior. In stamp and coin collecting it is the actual errors which are most highly prized, the stamps with lettering missing, the coins withdrawn from circulation because of technical inaccuracies. Dealers and auctioneers learn to recognize documented rarities and alter their prices accordingly, but the amateurs know so much more than the professionals in most of these subjects that, according to the collectors' crazy code of values, bargains abound in the trade.

Rarity collectors are a subdivision of the largest group of buyers in the art and antiques market after the followers of fashion. They combine the characteristics of narrower groups of collectors by taking an interest in rarity of marking as well as historical significance and physical appropriateness. To these interests they add a definite liking for aesthetic quality and a partiality to the social enjoyments of collecting. Such buyers often have a number of subjects in which they are forming collections at any one time, and their approach to antiques is similar to that of earlier generations. Eighteenth-century cognoscenti concentrated on what were actually known as 'cabinet collections', which comprised expanding bodies of material kept in cupboards and drawers, mostly in the library or study, and brought out of hiding for private inspection or for the intellectual appreciation of friends. In those days prints and water-colours were invariably kept in folio cabinets rather than on the walls, medals were deposited in velvet-lined drawers, and collections of fifteenth-century Limoges enamels were stored in purpose-built cabinets. These days a collector likes to have at least part of his collection on display in glass-fronted cabinets or on shelves, but the principle behind its formation is the same, namely to amass an unlimited amount of material in a given field.

Modern cognoscenti are always finding new fields of interest to be grafted on to the canons of acceptable taste. In the old days a classical education ensured that connoisseurs concentrated on antiquities and related antiquarian topics, but legitimate subjects for cabinet collecting now include tin-plate toys and callotypes, as well as established fields such as lacquer, ethnographica, and musical instruments. Societies have been formed to further the interests of numerous different groups of collectors; meetings and lectures are arranged on unheard-of topics; and the market has become attractively uninhibited and inventive.

There are also serious collectors who, rather than concentrating on a particular medium or manufacturer, prefer to define their interests by way of period or style. They are prepared to buy all kinds of artefacts in any medium, provided a significant stylistic point is made within their chosen period. Such collectors become very knowledgeable about many disciplines covering a relatively short period of time, as their interests normally extend beyond the decorative arts to the painting and architecture of the period as well. They may even design gardens in their favoured style and cook food with the appropriate period flavour to complement their furnishings. All this can become exaggeratedly arcane, especially when attempts are made to reproduce original lighting and the host dresses *en suite* with the decor – jellabas and fezes for the Ottoman collector, frock coats and cravats for the Victorian collector, silk dressing-gowns and long cigarette-holders for the Art Deco collector. With care taken to avoid meaningless theatricality, successful period collectors stimulate a far broader cultural appreciation than concentration on a single subject, albeit on a wider time-scale. The literature of the period will be understood and the music and sculpture appreciated instead of just the pottery and the wallpaper. This is a great improvement on some narrow specialists, both dealers and collectors, who are pitifully ignorant about other subjects and give the overall impression of being uninterested and uninformed about anything outside their speciality.

Another group of collectors are moved to buy only the oddities of the antiques market. Their homes look like warehouses belonging to film studios specializing in period melodramas. One of the maxims of the trade is that, provided you can find him, a buyer exists for everything, however outlandish; oddity collectors are the kind of people who cannot resist buying the object which no one else would accept as a gift. A pair of fairground horses gallop down the hall to collect the coats, a Passion Week crucifix holds the hats, and a stuffed bicephalous lamb grazes in the downstairs loo. One of the attractions of oddities is that they tend to be quite cheap, as after a week or two of customers' giggles at a Tibetan ceremonial ox harness the dealer begins to wonder why on earth he bought it and is happy to sell out at a knockdown price to the first person who shows any interest. But it is not merely the cheapness which attracts the oddity buyer, for many an unacceptably conventional bargain will be passed up in favour of a two-ton Georgian printing press for £100 including delivery to the garden shed, or a moulting ostrich-feather elephant switch for a fiver. There is seldom any room in suburban semis for ordinary functional works of art, and the oddities are put to unusual uses, a Gothic door from Cerne Abbas Monastery serving as a coffee table, a Victorian diver's helmet as a table lamp, or the Maharajah of Jaipur's baby carriage as a tea trolley.

The psychology of collecting has yet to receive detailed scientific analysis; since there are more significant and disruptive aspects of human nature deserving attention, collecting is rather superficially described as being one of the anal complexes. But whatever the underlying psychological impulses of the collector might be, the motivation to collect is often dangerously and self-destructively strong. It is difficult to avoid thinking of the collector's strength as basically negative when the passionate drive for acquisition of beautiful things turns in on itself, leading first to depression and then to suicide – the fate of too many dedicated collectors for mere coincidence. There is a touch of the macabre about the ruthless pursuit by collectors of the entrails of dead, discredited societies, and nothing necessarily admirable about antique dealers who are the potentially sinister agents in this unhealthy exercise. While fine collections on posthumous exhibition can give pleasure to the public, one of the primary motives in their formation is the guarded and personally possessive pleasure of ownership, another basically unsympathetic human characteristic. Intense competitiveness and bitter jealousy are kept under control by civilized collectors, but in some they surface in violent and despicable forms. And as has been suggested before, collecting is for others a way of escape from confrontation with the realities of life and of themselves. It is an unproductive way of escape in all but those exceptional circumstances when a collection of brilliant individuality illuminates the minds and warms the hearts of those who witness its creation.

The issues currently dominating coffee and cocktail conversations in the London trade loom large in the lives of dealers and auctioneers, minor though their impact may be on public consciousness. Many of the issues involve either threats to the capital security of the rich on whom the antiques market depends, or restrictions on the freedom of movement of works of art, the essential precondition of an expanding business. The interests of the dealers are contrary to those of the numerical majority of collectors who find themselves being priced out of the market; indeed the ordinary collector would benefit if all the dealers' worst fears came true and antiques ceased to become a tax- and currency-efficient form of capital investment. The imposition of taxes on the possession as well as on the disposal of works of art, and on their import and export, would frighten away people who buy because of fashion rather than through genuine interest, and the rich investors would quickly find some other financially advantageous market in which to bury their wealth safe from socialist attack. Many of the issues are therefore political – leading dealers and auctioneers are regimentally conservative in their politics.

As a member of the European Economic Community, Britain is being subjected to a certain amount of pressure to alter its position regarding the import and export of antiques in order to facilitate uniformity in the laws for the whole Common Market. The powerful Bond Street lobby has persuaded successive British governments to stand firm and put forward the argument that the rest of Europe should bring itself in line with the British tax authorities who operate the freest system of them all. With few exceptions, works of art more than fifty years old can be taken in and out of Britain with minimal documentation and zero taxation. An export licence must be obtained on works of art at a declared value higher than a given threshold, currently £8,000, but this exercise is seldom more than a formality. Companies registered in England and individual residents are supposed to remit the full sale proceeds of any work of art they export and do not reimport within the appropriate period. This official ruling is impossible to implement as the declared value accepted on export can easily be a quarter of the actual retail price, but customs and excise have no means of proving this and are usually obliged to accept remission of the lower export valuation.

Works of art considered to be of national importance can be refused an export licence for a limited period, within which time the government must supply or an institution must raise the required sum of money to buy the piece at the export price in order to prevent its leaving the country. All this is very different from the situation in France and Italy, where antiques are subject to import duties from both foreigners and nationals, and the government is empowered to refuse export licences at will. In France the laborious system of applying for export licences separately at two different offices of the Beaux Arts for all works of art, whatever their value, is in itself a costly and time-consuming disincentive to export, apart from the danger that an export licence will be refused indefinitely. On refusing an export licence, the government has no obligation to purchase but has the option to do so at an arbitrated price which may not necessarily reflect the true value. In Italy the officers of the Belle Arte have gone one step further by keeping a permanently updated list of the owners of 'notified' works of art which are considered to be part of the national heritage and can on no account leave the country. This system developed from the post-war listing of Italian art treasures in order to recover possessions looted by the Germans or hidden by the Resistance for safe-keeping. Welcomed then, notification is now feared by collectors, as confinement to the domestic market more than halves the value of an important piece. Works of art appearing in auction in Italy, in dealers' shops, or in export consignments can be added to the notified list instantly and virtually without argument, and an intricate network of illicit exporters has grown up in Italy to circumvent this danger.

Value Added Tax is another subject of disagreement within the European Community and an area where certain sections of the British trade fear parity with the Continent. The paper work involved in keeping correct accounts and stock books for the British tax authorities is laborious enough, but it is nothing compared with the complexity of the schemes invented by Italian dealers in order to avoid punitive import duties and the dreaded 'I.V.A.'. Difficulties in the British system of applying Value Added Tax arise from the unclear definition of 'antiques' for purposes of taxation and from the Bond Street lobby's success in persuading Customs and Excise to offer the option of a special antique dealer's scheme of V.A.T. payment on the margin of profit rather than on the total sale price. It would be much simpler for tax gatherers, taxpayers and even for the buyers if all antiques, whether sold at auction, in a retail shop or by direct supply, were subject to the automatic addition of a uniform V.A.T. like manufactured luxury goods. Under the 'special scheme' V.A.T. is not shown separately and cannot be claimed back by tax-registered museums or companies; this hidden tax does not have to be paid by the trader on works of art which are exported, thus giving dealers an added incentive to find buyers abroad for the country's ever-decreasing stock of historical mementoes.

Given the fact that successful London dealers and auctioneers are able to keep themselves so well groomed in dark blue mohair suits and gilt-buckled Gucci shoes by courtesy of the rich foreigners who do most of the buying, it is surprising in one way to find the trade such a solid opponent to increased death duties and the threatened wealth tax. The trade might have been expected to relish the forcing onto the market of masterpieces from the stately homes of our impoverished nobility, thus providing more fine things for them to sell abroad to their carefully trained millionaire customers. The reason for the trade's objection is that the imposition of a wealth tax on land, houses, works of art and other possessions would squeeze collectors all the way down the line and prices in the domestic market would be decimated overnight. Worse still, the dealers and auctioneers would themselves be forced to sell some of the treasures from their own homes in order to pay their taxes on the remainder. With so many fine things flooding onto the market, collectors could pick and choose in which Grinling Gibbons looking glass they wished to regard themselves, and prices for almost everything would plummet.

Forever dissatisfied, the trade is currently complaining about prices being too high rather than too low, and difficult times are forecast now that the Getty millions have been allowed by the American courts to flow freely into the coffers of the dead tycoon's Malibu museum. Dark doom itself is envisaged if the British Rail Pension Fund, Shaikh Whoever or anyone else should decide to compete in the market place with the John Paul Getty Museum – it is feared that no dealer could ever again afford to buy anything good in open competition. Now that the British Rail Pension Fund has temporarily stopped spending train drivers' savings on Tiepolo drawings, some of the controversy surrounding the agency of a London firm of auctioneers in this activity has died down. At the time, however, dealers were incensed by an auctioneer's negotiating this exclusive contract to advise the biggest single buyer in the market. The auctioneer, as agent to the seller, cannot pretend to act independently for the buyer as well, and the auction rooms must inevitably tend to recommend works of art in their own sales before rival auction material or dealers' stock. Furthermore, the thought of competing City institutions passing magnificent works of art from one underground vault to another like bundles of share certificates is an unpleasant vision of the art market of the future, but it is not so far removed from the aim of some advisers to the British Rail Pension Fund.

One way or another, auction practice is always a bone of contention with dealers. The buyer's premium is today's talking point, though it will soon cease to be so as the trade has chosen not to challenge the legality of raising a charge for a service which, some would say, cannot be supplied. Like many other issues, the premium will soon become accepted practice and dealers will be pleasantly surprised when buying at one of the provincial auction houses which does not add a fat 10 per cent tip to the bill. Only gross inefficiency can prevent the making of large profits by a selling agent who takes the 25 per cent commission on lots under £500 as currently charged by one of the largest auction houses in London. This fact goes some way to explaining why American financiers are so keen on owning an international auction house. But the dealers have not lost all their battles, for auctioneers no longer dare purchase works of art on their own account as frequently as they did in the early 1970s, and better systems have been devised for accounts and other after-sales services.

Antiques fairs have recently become an issue in the trade. At certain months of the year dealers seem intent on fighting among themselves as rival fairs of massive proportions vie for publicity and for customers. A deep rift has also appeared in ruling circles of the British Antique Dealers' Association over the relative prestige of the two annual events of greatest portent, the revived jamboree at the

Grosvenor House, and the sophisticated affair supported by the Royal Academy at Burlington House.

At the other end of the scale, the legality has been questioned of those Sunday antiques fairs which are mounted every week up and down the country. Even if it turns out that they do not contravene the Sunday trading laws, fairs of this kind might as well be avoided anyway because of the appallingly high percentage of rubbish being peddled by ignorant amateurs.

The practicalities of consumer protection have commanded considerable attention within the trade now for some years. The three leading dealers' organizations, the British Antique Dealers' Association (B.A.D.A.), the London and Provincial Antique Dealers Association (L.A.P.A.D.A.) and the Society of London Art Dealers (S.L.A.D.), take pains to point out to collectors that buyers in shops can call on the considerable powers of the Trades Description Acts and the Sale of Goods Acts to protect their interest, whereas buyers at auction have few, if any, rights at law. The conditions of sale posted and published by most auction houses specifically exclude responsibility for the accuracy of catalogue descriptions, and while leading companies choose to protect their reputations by returning the purchase price on out-and-out fakes, they emphasize that all descriptions are to be taken as a statement of opinion, not of fact. Furthermore, auctioneers shelter under the storm-proof legal umbrella of function as agents rather than principals, which means that they are absolved from all legal obligations to the buyer despite the fact that they impose a buyer's premium defined by Customs and Excise as a service charge. The Law Commissions of 1969 and 1975 were in deep disagreement about the general position of the auctioneer, but they did make recommendations on one important point. Even when selling as an agent it was made clear that the auctioneer is bound to prove the 'reasonableness' of his exclusion clauses rather than the buyer having to prove their '*un*reasonableness'. Sadly, the Commission did not give an opinion on the established convention that the one thing an auctioneer means when describing a picture as painted by 'Rubens' is that it is definitely not in his opinion the work of Rubens himself, indeed was not even executed during the painter's lifetime. Even when the auctioneer describes a painting as being by 'Sir Peter Paul Rubens', prints a detailed historical dissertation on its importance, publishes an estimate of its value at a million pounds, and strongly advises a client to buy it at that price or more, the auctioneer still claims complete immunity from the normal breach of contract laws if the picture turns out to be a nineteenth-century copy. The so-called guarantee of authenticity, which is denied at various points in the conditions of sale, refers only to works of art made to deceive, not to school works or originally harmless copies and reproductions. A rich, public-spirited collector may one day decide to challenge in court the 'reasonableness' of these conventional exclusion clauses under the Unfair Contract Terms Act of 1977.

At some smaller auction houses yet stranger conventions of description abound. The letters 'a.f.', standing for 'as found', tacked on to the end of a catalogue description, mean that the buyer is obliged to accept the piece in whatever precarious condition it might happen to be. Use of the letters 's.a.f.', 'slightly as found', is to be interpreted as meaning that the piece is damaged to a lesser degree. Experienced auctiongoers have learnt that catalogues seldom list chips, cracks and faults for fear of offending their vendors, and the letters 'a.f.' are in effect a secret code to regular buyers warning them that the jardinière or whatever is actually unusable and unrepairable. There is very little a disappointed buyer at auction can do about these undoubtedly misleading conventions, or about missed bids by the auctioneer and other frustrations of the rooms.

When buying from dealers, on the other hand, collectors have absolutely clear contractual rights which can be enforced in the courts if necessary. It is beyond argument, for example, that if a dealer puts a ticket on a bureau saying simply 'Queen Anne' then the buyer can demand his money back if the piece of furniture turns out not to have been made in England in the early eighteenth century. He can also sue for legal costs, for certain damages and for interest on the sum of money involved. Under the Trade Descriptions Act even a verbal opinion that the bureau is 'Queen Anne' is enough; though it is obviously easier to prove the case when buyers can produce a detailed written invoice to the effect, and no reputable dealer will deny this to a buyer. The buyer has the same right to rescind the contract should a table described as being made of oak actually be constructed of beech, or if a chair should collapse because of its battered condition – it is no use the dealer's saying that the type of wood makes no difference to the price, or that the 'merchantable quality' of antiques cannot be guaranteed, because by legal definition an antique chair is made for sitting on just as a new chair is and if this is not possible the dealer must take back his unsuable article and repay the buyer.

A recent court ruling ordered a British dealer to repay to a client not only the original purchase price of $18,000 for a 'fake' but also a further $23,000 in interest plus £10,000 legal costs. The Limitations Act of 1980 suggests that a dealer's responsibility lapses after six years unless the buyer can

successfully argue that he could not have proved the mistake by using 'reasonable diligence' within the given period. In this case, the court order for interest and expenses was made thirteen years after the original sale even though the dealer had offered to repay the purchase price immediately the article was discovered to be a reproduction eleven years after he had sold it to the collector.

Art market escapades of this kind offer a salutary reminder of the essential vulnerability of a trade whose practitioners, the auctioneers and the dealers, loudly and steadfastly claim is as safe as the brokerage of long-term British government bonds, and far more profitable. The 'fake' in the recent court case had been authenticated by the Louvre and exhibited at the Grand Palais as an important drawing by Ingres; it was subsequently highly valued as such for insurance by a leading London auction house before it was eventually removed from its Victorian frame and seen to be a rather obvious photographic reproduction. In this instance there was no intention to deceive, either in the original manufacture of the object or in its subsequent retailing. It is, nevertheless, a poor reflection on the trade when, as frequently happens in all fields, mechanically produced copies made by previous generations for purely decorative purposes are bought and sold as the original masterpieces. Collectors might ask themselves why they pay so much money for Ingres drawings when neither they nor the experts can see the difference in a valueless photographic reproduction.

The making and marketing of fakes, works of art intended to deceive, is a criminal offence as opposed to the civil offence of handling fakes or reproductions by mistake. Some forgers are motivated by a desire to embarrass the artistic elite and, like Tom Keating, may not be interested in

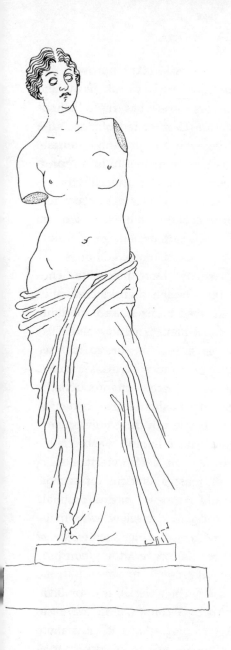

financial profit. Most people who make fakes, however, and those who market them are motivated by making money. The most successful forgeries are those which reproduce the manner of the original artist or designer rather than those which are made as direct copies, but in the antiques trade most of the fakes on the market are neither of these hand-made artefacts; they are mass-produced manufactured casts taken from original examples. The quality of these reproductions is often so dire and the look of the synthetic material so different from the original medium that the hope of deception might seem forlorn. Yet tens of thousands of people every year are caught by plastic Art Deco dancers pretending to be bronze and ivory statuettes, cold cast resin retrievers trying to be animalier bronzes, and moulded soapstone passion flowers sold as Chien Lung jade. The simple explanation of this is greed, the desire to have something for nothing which persuades normally prudent individuals that street market reproductions are actually bargain originals. Some dealers who should know better are caught in the same way and cringe with embarrassment when the obvious is pointed out to them by a more level-headed friend in the trade. As the cost both of making individual forgeries and of mass-producing commercial fakes is considerable, it only happens once fashionable demand has pushed prices up to a level which can be undercut at a profit. In today's uncritical scramble for antiques the list of known areas of forgery grows month by month and includes bronzes, netsuke, scrimshaw, mirrors, stamps, coins, manuscripts, kneehole desks, memorabilia, jade, Art Nouveau, glass, Art Deco statues, ethnographica, campaign chests, snuff boxes, photographs, and much more besides the well-known scandals in the picture market perpetrated by such as Jan van Meegeren and David Stein.

Dealers like to make light of these art market upsets and dismiss press reports of malpractice as the idle gossip of column-starved journalists. The astonishing strength of today's international art market is built on public confidence, and dealers will go to any lengths with their allies in the auction rooms to protect this image of propriety. Rich clients must remain convinced that their money is safe when stored in rococo commodes. If there is any indication of change in the market then the direction of change must be upwards and outwards; dealers pray as hard as the auctioneers themselves for record prices in the season's leading sales, so that the increase in the value of antiques can somehow be demonstrated to have inflation and devaluation beaten. Blind confidence is placed in the belief that the popularity of antiques is a definitive characteristic of civilized society – so long as capitalism exists, it is argued by the trade, new people will appear on the scene to stoke the market, and no one need fear for their investments if they buy well.

Most dealers have learnt the trick of confidence but they are not all confidence tricksters, for the trade does, by and large, promote works of art of intrinsic quality and interest. The fact that many clients understand little of what they are buying will never tempt a good dealer to become a quack doctor and sell sugared pills instead of real medicine. Older dealers may bewail the passing of those 'gentlemanly' times when antiques were bought and sold among the few. In truth, the glare of television spotlights and the investigative persistence of journalists have forced more open and accountable practices onto the trade, which may now be less 'gentlemanly' but is probably more honest. The more that is known by the public about the secretive practices of dealers and auctioneers, the more solidly based the market will become. Lack of external regulation and the traditional tolerance within the trade of shady deals have encouraged unscrupulous and uncritical individuals into the business, and it is this kind of dealer who suffers under public accountability. Good dealers have nothing to hide, indeed their historical knowledge and business flair will be properly admired by comparison with the feebleness or crookedness of others.

Letting collectors into some of the secrets of the trade should not be seen as a threat to decent dealers or to the trade in general. Collectors need to feel confident in their participation in the trade, and knowledge of how dealers work will increase their confidence. More than that, though the motives for collecting are varied they have a single central strand in common, the seeking of personal satisfaction in whatever form that might be found. There is no moral justification for collecting antiques and it is far from being a social necessity or human right, but it is something which can be enjoyed by many people in a number of different ways. The more people know about 'antiques' and antique dealers the more genuine will be their enjoyment of the dangerously fashionable pastime of 'collecting'.

Index

Index